To Lynn—
an Austin stalwart
—Red Wassenich

KEEPING AUSTIN WEIRD

DEDICATION

TO KAREN PAVELKA, LIGHT OF MY LIFE

KEEPING AUSTIN WEIRD

A Guide to the (Still) Odd Side of Town

Text and Photography by Red Wassenich
Illustrations by Penny Van Horn

Schiffer Publishing Ltd

4880 Lower Valley Road • Atglen, PA 19310

OTHER SCHIFFER BOOKS BY RED WASSENICH

KEEP AUSTIN WEIRD
A GUIDE TO THE ODD SIDE OF TOWN
978-0-7643-2639-4

OTHER SCHIFFER BOOKS ON RELATED SUBJECTS

HAUNTED AUSTIN, TEXAS
SCOTT A. JOHNSON
978-0-7643-3298-2

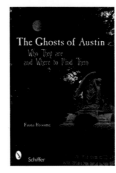

THE GHOSTS OF AUSTIN, TEXAS
WHO THE GHOSTS ARE AND WHERE TO FIND THEM
FIONA BROOME
978-0-7643-2680-6

For our complete selection of fine books on this and related subjects, please visit our website at www.schifferbooks.com. You may also write for a free catalog.

Schiffer Publishing's titles are available at special discounts for bulk purchases for sales promotions or premiums. Special editions, including personalized covers, corporate imprints, and excerpts, can be created in large quantities for special needs. For more information, contact the publisher.

We are always looking for people to write books on new and related subjects. If you have an idea for a book, please contact us at proposals@schifferbooks.com

LIBRARY OF CONGRESS CONTROL NUMBER: 2015958031

TYPE SET IN HELVETICA & MEANWHILE

ISBN: 978-0-7643-5096-2
PRINTED IN CHINA

PHOTOGRAPHY © RED WASSENICH.
ILLUSTRATIONS © PENNY VAN HORN, PAGES 36, 47, 74, 121

PUBLISHED BY SCHIFFER PUBLISHING, LTD.
4880 LOWER VALLEY ROAD
ATGLEN, PA 19310
PHONE: (610) 593-1777; FAX: (610) 593-2002
E-MAIL: INFO@SCHIFFERBOOKS.COM
WEB: WWW.SCHIFFERBOOKS.COM

CONTENTS

INTRODUCTION

Keep Austin Weird was born in the spring of 2000, so it has entered its troubled teen years: confused, torn between trying to fit in and trying to find its own identity. Is it still weird? Is it OK to be changing? What's all this strange growth?

The phrase originally fell out of my mouth while calling in a donation to KOOP radio, during my favorite segment, "The Lounge Show," which plays smooth crooners and plenty of other oddball music—if you haven't heard Bing Crosby's "Hey, Jude" you haven't lived. (Happily, it's still on 10 a.m. to noon on Saturdays.) When asked why I was donating to the show, I said, "It helps keep Austin weird." A tiny cartoon light bulb ignited.

I mentioned the phrase to my wife, Karen Pavelka, who ordered bumper stickers, and I set up the website (keepaustinweird. com). We began a glacial grassroots campaign, handing out the bumper stickers to those we thought worthy.

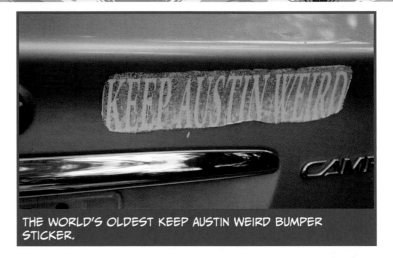

THE WORLD'S OLDEST KEEP AUSTIN WEIRD BUMPER STICKER.

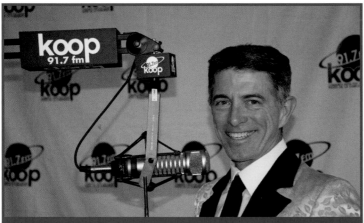

JAY ROBILLARD, DJ OF "THE LOUNGE SHOW," WHICH WAS THE MUSE FOR THE INVENTION OF THE PHRASE KEEP AUSTIN WEIRD. JAY MATCHES THE SMOOTH TUNES HE HAS SPUN SINCE 1994.

STEVE BERCU OF BOOKPEOPLE AND JOHN KUNZ OF WATERLOO RECORDS ARE GUILTY OF MUCH OF KEEP AUSTIN WEIRD'S SUCCESS.

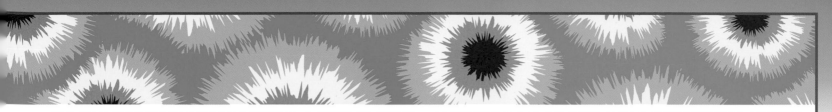

THE PHRASE IS A MARKETING MAINSTAY NOWADAYS.

BEING WEIRD BECOMES A MACHO BRAG.

It slowly gained traction after a couple of years and it really caught lightning in a bottle when BookPeople and Waterloo Records used the phrase—with "Support Local Business" tacked on—as part of a protest against a proposed city $2.1 million incentive for a mega Borders Books to be built right across the street, a development that almost assuredly would have led to the death of both local, iconic businesses. They handed out free bumper stickers with the phrase and their logos. As of this writing they have given away over 200,000. The city of Austin wisely backed out of their incentive offer, and the two local businesses are doing well (and Borders went belly up in 2011).

ACCORDING TO THE *AUSTIN BUSINESS JOURNAL*, IN 2014, 36,196 "KEEP AUSTIN WEIRD" T-SHIRTS WERE SOLD JUST AT THE AUSTIN AIRPORT. SINCE THEY GO FOR ABOUT $25 A POP, THE SCHMUCKS AT OUTHOUSE DESIGN, WHO TRADEMARKED THE PHRASE FOR SHIRTS AND HATS, SHOULD BE SO PROUD OF THEIR CREATION...OH, UH....

Another source of the phrase's fame grew out my (unsuccessful) fight against Outhouse Design when they filed for trademark use of the phrase on shirts and hats. The kerfuffle was covered in the *Austin American-Statesman* and *The New York Times*.

Most people likely think of the phrase as primarily a marketing phrase, which hadn't crossed my mind when creating it. I certainly endorse the buy-local movement and I'm proud it helped—see Weird Businesses, page 122—but my perspective comes from a street-level fondness for goofy, anachronistic, unserious, unmaterialistic bohemianism. Also from my inflated ego.

THE BIG QUESTION

So, the elephant in the condo: Is Austin still weird? Yes. But it is very threatened, primarily by the influx of money, which is generally a prophylactic against weirdness. The phrase was born and grew out of these same forces that threatened the weirdness in 2000—a boom-town, go-go aura that was suffusing the slacker, eccentric, smallish city. The same is happening again, now that the 2008 recession has faded. Rents rose fifty percent from 2004 to 2013. Austin has the highest cost of living in Texas; it used to have the lowest. According to a 2015 study, it is the most economically segregated large city in the United States. Restaurants serving foam of duck's breath as an *amuse-bouche* flourish.

I have noticed a definite trend. Old timers here bemoan the end of Austin's weirdness. Newcomers love it here and are struck by our town's singular personality. David Heymann,

A MILD EXAMPLE OF GENTRIFICATION ON THE EAST SIDE. GOOD-BYE CHEAP HOUSING.

University of Texas architecture professor and author of the novel *My Beautiful City Austin*, put it well: "It doesn't matter if you've been here five years or 50 years, Austin has gotten worse. It doesn't matter when you got here: That was its best point, the best you've ever seen it. It just keeps getting worse." Hmmm, I was born here. So it has all been downhill for six decades.

But don't worry, I'm not going to whine about the good ol' days … much. In doing this book, a follow-up to my *Keep Austin Weird: A Guide to the Odd Side of Town*, I was happily relieved to find the state of the city still weird. But eternal eccentricity is the price we must pay to save the weirdness. Do your part!

AUSTIN UNDER THE MICROSCOPE

Every time you look, Austin is being named to some best-of, worst-of, most-of list. Best for business, worst for traffic, drunkest city, and, of course, the one that is the basis of our official city motto, the 250-plus venues that make us the Live Music Capital of the World.

According to the influential urban scholar Richard Florida, our emphasis on the arts, design, high tech, research, and education make us a top-level city. His book *The Rise of the Creative Class* in 2002 pegged Austin as being in the forefront, thus explaining its boomtown status among the hipoisie. This analysis led to a blue-ribbon, widely read white paper (please note the patriotic theme I just invoked) on economic development from the Austin city government extolling the virtues of weirdness. The so-called "Keep Austin Weird" study seems to have led more to development than to weirdness, but it could easily be worse. I reluctantly admit I'd rather live in an era of development than one of rot.

A GOVERNMENT WITH ITS PRIORITIES RIGHT.

DR. JOSH LONG, AUTHOR OF THE ENTERTAINING AND INFORMATIVE ANALYSIS OF AUSTIN, WEIRD CITY, AT SPIDER HOUSE.

The winner of the most tiresome analysis is a UT dissertation titled "Everyday Intensities: Rhetorical Theory, Composition Studies, and the Affective Field of Culture," which in its abstract (an appropriate word) says, "While the Keep Austin Weird movement can be seen as a rhetorical response to the 'exigence' of city-wide overdevelopment, we can also situate the exigence's evocation within a wider context of affective ecologies comprised of ongoing processes of material experiences, stories, moods, and public feelings." Wow! I did not know that was the point.

In happily stark contrast is another dissertation—published in 2010 by UT Press as a real book—*Weird City: Sense of Place and Creative Resistance in Austin, Texas*, by Josh Long. This professor at Southwestern University in the orbiting city of Georgetown

LET'S LOOK AT THE NUMBERS. A ZANDAN POLL OF AUSTINITES IN SPRING 2015 HAD THESE FIGURES:

IS AUSTIN WEIRD? 69% YES

ARE YOU WEIRD? 40% YES

WHAT SLOGAN BEST REPRESENTS THE AUSTIN OF TODAY? "KEEP AUSTIN WEIRD" 29% (1ST PLACE)

wrote with the rare combination of academic soundness and enjoyable readability. Josh interviewed me for his dissertation, and we have become friends. Buy it, read it. It has a fresh, complex analysis of Austin.

UNCREATIVE CITIES

A large number of cities have "borrowed" Keep Wherever Weird. It seems a bit ironic that cities proclaiming their uniqueness would go the cookie-cutter route, but let's not get haughty. As he openly admits, BookPeople owner Steve Bercu is responsible for most of these due to his frequent speaking appearances around the country on behalf of supporting local businesses.

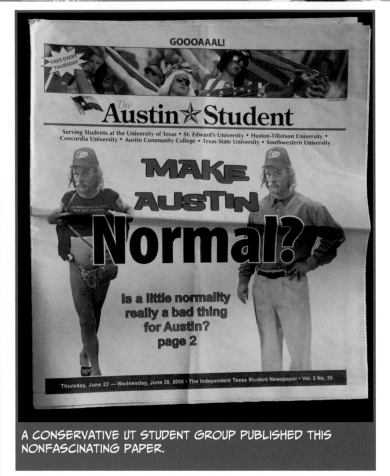

A CONSERVATIVE UT STUDENT GROUP PUBLISHED THIS NONFASCINATING PAPER.

The most prominent is Keep Portland Weird, due both to a sign shown at the beginning of the TV series *Portlandia* and to the competition between the two cities to be the edgiest.

There's a little-known Google search trick where you put a phrase in quotation marks and put an asterisk or two in place of a word or words (called a "wildcard"). The search "keep * weird" gets about 200,000,000 results, so have at if you're obsessive.

Some of the places that have adopted the mantra seem like a major stretch: Gulfport, Florida; Knoxville, Tennessee; Chico, California; Washington, DC; America; the World.

It should be noted that, unbeknownst to me, evidently there was a short-lived Keep Erie Weird campaign in the early 1980s as a mock protest against a rise in beer prices. They revived it not too long ago, but I always get stuck on why in hell they didn't say Keep Erie Eerie.

Other towns have riffed on the phrase in creative ways, such as Keep San Antonio Lame, Keep Dallas Plastic and Keep Dallas Pretentious, Keep Lubbock Flat, etc. My favorite is Albuquerque's Keep It Querque.

Austin's primary 'burb neighbor has codified their fondness for blandness with Keep Round Rock Normal. And another town wedged between the two cities countered with: Pflugerville: Between a Rock and a Weird Place.

Then there's the rather tiresome attempt Make Austin Normal. It seems to be pretty quiescent, but for a while it vigorously flogged junk with slogans like "Buy from Chain Stores." Irony done with a sledgehammer.

IN THE BEGINNING THERE WAS THE WORD

Weird is a weird word. First off, it violates the schoolroom dictum of "i before e, except after c or when it sounds like a in 'neighbor' or 'weigh.'" (There are, as of 2015, over 200,000 Google results for the phrase "keep austin weird," but there are an additional 4,700 for "keep austin wierd.")

It has a wacky etymology, too. The Old English *wyrd* meant "destiny." This morphed (or is it phonemed?) into the Middle English *werd*, which moved the definition more into the occult. The Holinshed Chronicles had the Werd Sisters as fortune tellers; Shakespeare had the Weird Sisters in *Macbeth* as a trio of strange witches. (Austin has the Weird Sisters Women's Theatre Collective.) Through what was probably a long series of typos, we ended up with today's spelling and the meaning also evolved to its current one of oddness.

A WEIRDO BY ANY OTHER NAME...
WOULD IT HAVE MADE ANY DIFFERENCE IF THE PHRASE HAD BEEN ONE OF THESE?

KEEP AUSTIN ODD
KEEP AUSTIN UNUSUAL
KEEP AUSTIN BIZARRE
KEEP AUSTIN SCREWY
KEEP AUSTIN LOCO
KEEP AUSTIN ECCENTRIC
KEEP AUSTIN KOOKY
KEEP AUSTIN OFF-KILTER
KEEP AUSTIN OUTRÉ
KEEP AUSTIN UNCANNY
KEEP AUSTIN THESAURUSED

Clamoring for weirdness is to laud a form of mental illness. The Keep Austin Weird idea is, I suspect, based on the premise that conventionality stifles creativity, that it is the goofballs who enjoy life most and also do the most ultimately to advance society. Only a child can believe such sentimentalistic drivel. But then, the Sixties turned America into a land of perpetual childhood. You are a suitable poster child.

FAN MAIL FROM SOME FLOUNDER.

"TEXAS' CAPITAL, WHERE COUNTLESS T-SHIRTS BEAR THE NOW QUAINTLY OUTDATED SLOGAN 'KEEP AUSTIN WEIRD.'"
—2014 ARTICLE IN *AMERICAN SONGWRITER*

THE CITY'S BUS SYSTEM GOT ON BOARD.

A LOW POINT IN THE HISTORY OF KEEP AUSTIN WEIRD SPINOFFS OCCURRED IN MAY 2015 WHEN THE AWFUL, UNFUNNY, RIGHT-WING COMIC STRIP *MALLARD FILLMORE* HAD A POINTY-HEADED LIBERAL HOLDING A PLACARD SAYING "KEEP HILLARY WEIRD!!"

So now let us look at the hard evidence. This book attempts to show a wide sampling of what your should-be humble author considers weird. I missed much, no doubt. Please inundate me with your nominees. Contact me at keepaustinweird@keepaustinweird.com and please visit the website.

CHAPTER 1
WEIRD PLACES

SOME SAY AUSTIN IS JUST A PERFORMANCE ARTWORK. THIS CANDID SHOT OF AN "OLD" DOWNTOWN BUILDING IS OFFERED AS EVIDENCE THAT THIS IS ALL A SPECIAL-EFFECTS TOWN.

DOWNTOWN IS A CONTRAST IN ARCHITECTURE. HERE A GORGEOUS PARKING GARAGE IS BURDENED BY BEING NEXT TO THE HIDEOUS OLD MILLET OPERA HOUSE (1878), NOW THE AUSTIN CLUB.

We are our environment. If that's true, we are turning into condos, so we better appreciate the loony places we still have. These range from entire neighborhoods to individual yards. Some are self-consciously going for the image (South Congress), while others do it instinctually, with no desire for recognition. The general realm of "places" is where gentrification rears its rear most starkly.

THE CATHEDRAL OF JUNK

Folks often ask me what's the weirdest thing in Austin. Happily there's an easy answer: The Cathedral of Junk. This three-story, sixty-ton behemoth in South Austin is the masterwork of visionary Vince Hannemann, who started it way back in 1989. More than 700 bicycles, for one example, blend with car parts, golf clubs, old computers, surfboards, you name it, to create a miraculously sturdy structure, built for exploration. In 2010, one humorless neighbor sicced the city code enforcers on him. Some pro bono lawyers and engineers got the city to back down, and the resulting media coverage made the code wonks look the fools. The Cathedral was found sound, despite being held together mainly with wire, no welds. This is all in Vince's backyard and years of constant visitors are getting a bit much. It's well worth a visit, but a prior appointment (and a reasonable donation) are a must. Google the name to find contact info.

THE MAD GENIUS VANCE HANNEMANN, CREATOR OF THE CATHEDRAL OF JUNK.

ANOTHER AREA JUST WAITING TO BE CONDOIZED IS THE BREMOND BLOCK ON WEST 7TH STREET. ALMOST A DOZEN DUMPS LIKE THIS FROM THE NINETEENTH CENTURY OCCUPY VALUABLE TURF.

THE GENERALLY INTENSE DECORATION YIELDS TO AN AIRY AERIE.

THE CATHEDRAL IS THREE STORIES TALL AND WEIGHS OVER SIXTY TONS.

MANY OF THE 700 BICYCLES IN THE CATHEDRAL ARE IN THIS TOWER.

ONE CAN STARE AT A SQUARE YARD FOR AN HOUR AND STILL SEE NEW THINGS.

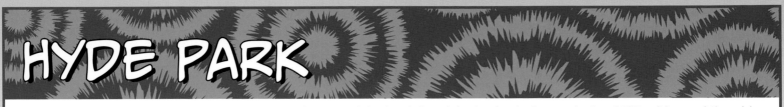

HYDE PARK

Hyde Park is the most beautiful neighborhood in town. It is Austin's original suburb, begun in the 1890s. Many of the older houses have quirky architecture, cost a fortune, and sit next to rundown student hovels, just the way God planned it.

SHIPE HOUSE IN HYDE PARK.

THE SHIPE HOUSE
MONROE MARTIN SHIPE (b. 1847) HAD THIS RESIDENCE BUILT IN 1892 IN AUSTIN'S HYDE PARK, A SUBURB WHICH HE DEVELOPED ON THE SITE OF THE OLD STATE FAIRGROUNDS. A MAN OF BROAD VISION, SHIPE BROUGHT INNOVATIVE CHANGES TO THE CITY'S FORM OF GOVERNMENT, ITS PUBLIC TRANSPORTATION SYSTEM, AND OTHER MATTERS OF CIVIC CONCERN. HIS HOME, PARTIALLY CONSTRUCTED OF WOOD FROM THE FAIR GRANDSTAND, STANDS AS A MONUMENT TO HIS ACHIEVEMENTS.
RECORDED TEXAS HISTORIC LANDMARK—1

SPARKY PARK

Hyde Park is home to a great little spot of tomfoolery: Sparky Park. Built as an electricity substation in the 1930s—a duty it gave up long ago—it remained as a half-acre hidden park. In 2008, the city unleashed the talents of artists Berthold and Emily Haas, who built an eccentricity substation by surrounding ugly modern electrical infrastructure with wonder walls. 3701 Grooms St., austinparks.org/our-parks.html?parkid=692.

CLARKSVILLE

Your author is fortunate to live in the Clarksville area, the closest residential neighborhood west of downtown. (Purists will chide me if I didn't point out that the true Clarksville is a specific tract within the Old West Austin neighborhood.) Clarksville has an interesting history. It was settled by freed slaves from the nearby Pease plantation and ended up as an African-American enclave in segregated Austin, where people of color lived in east Austin. It also morphed into something of a hippie enclave in the '60s and '70s due to the low rents and a progressive vibe. Sadly only a handful of African American households remain, but the left-wingers hang on. In the 2000 presidential election, the Old West Austin local precinct voted native son George W. Bush third behind Al Gore and Ralph Nader.

THE HASKELL HOUSE IS A PRESERVED EXAMPLE OF A FREED SLAVE'S HOME IN CLARKSVILLE. THIS 500-SQUARE-FOOT HOUSE WOULD GO FOR ABOUT $500,000 THESE DAYS. I WISH I WERE KIDDING.

ODD NEIGHBORHOODS

THIS QUIRKY RESIDENCE IS IN THE NORTH UNIVERSITY NEIGHBORHOOD, WHICH BORDERS HYDE PARK.

A CHARMING BIT OF COMMUNISM IN THE OLD WEST AUSTIN NEIGHBORHOOD FIRST APPEARED IN AN ALLEY IN 2014. SEVERAL HOUSEHOLDS GROW HERBS AND VEGETABLES TO SHARE WITH PASSERSBY.

THE NICE IF SOMEWHAT STEPFORD-LIKE MUELLER NEIGHBORHOOD, FORMER LOCATION OF THE AIRPORT, HAS STREETS ALL NAMED AFTER LOCAL HEROES.

IN A TRIBUTE TO ALFRED HITCHCOCK, A FLOCK OF MONK PARAKEETS—COMMONLY CALLED PARROTS—HAS INVADED SEVERAL AUSTIN LOCATIONS. EASILY IDENTIFIABLE BY THEIR SQUAWKS, GREEN FEATHERS, AND TRENDY CHOICE OF LIVING IN CONDOS, THEIR HUGE GROUP NESTS ADORN MANY CELL-PHONE TOWERS AND STADIUM LIGHT STANDARDS.

THE SANTA RITA RIG

This event is not normally thought of as weird, but it's always held the same time as SXSW, so the culture clash does spark.

THE SANTA RITA RIG ON THE SOUTH EDGE OF THE UT CAMPUS IS AN HOMAGE TO THE SOURCE OF THE UNIVERSITY'S MASSIVE ENDOWMENT—BLACK GOLD, TEXAS TEA. PERIODICALLY, IT BEGINS TO QUITE LOUDLY TELL ITS OWN STORY, WHICH I CAN TELL YOU FROM PERSONAL EXPERIENCE HAS VERY MUCH SURPRISED MANY A STONED STUDENT PASSING BY.

THE WEIRD HOMES TOUR

The Weird Homes Tour began in 2014. It features a wide variety of abodes, from dumpsters to grand, if odd, homes. The following is a sampling. Visit weirdhomestour.com for upcoming expeditions.

Austin
WEiRd HOME
tour

1 James at Casa Neverlandia
305 Milton Street West, 78704

2 Darryl at the Artists Retreat
7912 Tisdale Drive, 78757

3 Stephanie at Flamingo Ranch
402 El Paso Street, 78704

4 Professor Dumpster Dr. Jeff
900 Chicon Street, Suite D, 78702

5 Bill's Earthbag House
1212 E. 10th Street, 78702

6 Shay at Tiny House
60 East Avenue, 78701

7 Zach at Rancho Burrito
1020 Linden Street, 78702

8 Lorne and Sterling at Eponymous Garden
1202 Garden Street, 78702

Brought to you by:

CASA NEVERLANDIA

Casa Neverlandia—one of the stops on the Weird Homes Tour—is the product of James Talbot's dedication to whimsical beauty and sustainability and is a cornerstone of Austin weirdness. This early twentieth-century, one-story house has been transformed into a towering three-story castle, with all sorts of witty and gorgeous features. Talbot's pantheism shows in his living room's division into areas celebrating fire, water, earth, and air. The entire interior flows with undulating plasterwork and touches of mosaics. (Talbot's mosaic work adorns the pedestrian walkways at the Austin airport. Also see page 65 in the Weird Art chapter.) There's a separate tower in back, connected by a slightly frightening truss-and-chain walkway. You can then slide down a fire pole. No heating or air conditioning, a composting toilet, solar panels, and a rain collection system are inarguable proof of Talbot's dedication to sustainability. Call to arrange a tour for a small fee by the genial host. See talbotworld.com.

JAMES TALBOT, THE WONDERFULLY ODD CREATOR OF NEVERLANDIA (WHO WOULD WANT THE CONTRIBUTION OF HIS EX-PARTNER, KAY PILS, ACKNOWLEDGED), STANDS IN THE ROOM DISPLAYING HIS INTRICATE, BEAUTIFUL BEADWORK. HE IS ALSO AN ARCHITECT, WITH A SPECIALTY IN PLAYSCAPES.

THE GREAT ROOM HOSTS PARTIES AND CONCERTS. HERE IT'S SET UP FOR PING PONG WHERE THE PLAYERS MUST WEAR COSTUMES AND USE THINGS LIKE TENNIS RACQUETS OR TOYS FOR PADDLES.

CASA NEVERLANDIA AMUSINGLY LOOMS OVER AN ORDINARY SOUTH AUSTIN NEIGHBORHOOD.

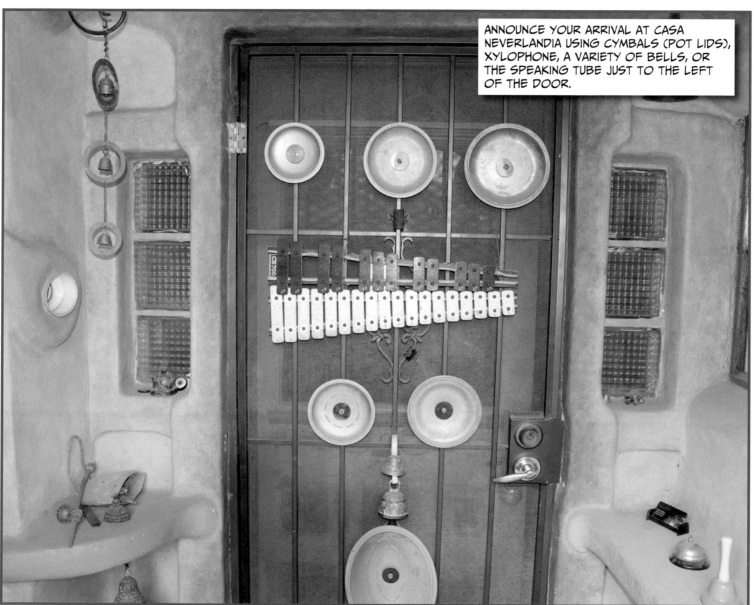

ANNOUNCE YOUR ARRIVAL AT CASA NEVERLANDIA USING CYMBALS (POT LIDS), XYLOPHONE, A VARIETY OF BELLS, OR THE SPEAKING TUBE JUST TO THE LEFT OF THE DOOR.

THE LIVING ROOM'S FIREPLACE IS A MONUMENT TO, UH, FIRE, WHILE DIRECTLY OPPOSITE IS THE ONE TO EARTH.

THE CASTLE

Another Weird Homes Tour stop was the castle built by Lisa Chronister and Elliot Johnson in the western part of Austin. This cast-earth structure with many sustainable features may seem more or less normal when you approach it, but inside it's highly crafted craziness, largely constructed by them personally. Their love of fantasy fiction shows in many touches, including mounted fictional animal carcasses. The house has been featured in many magazines, both for its whimsy and its innovative construction.

LISA AND ELLIOT DON'T TRY TO HIDE THEIR SKELETON IN A CLOSET.

A "GREEN MAN" FIREPLACE IN THE LIVING ROOM OF THE ELLIOTT-CHRONISTER WEIRD HOME.

IMAGINARY ANIMALS ARE THE RESULTS OF IMAGINARY SAFARIS. LISA'S EXCELLENT STAINED-GLASS WORK ADDS TO THE DREAMLIKE QUALITY OF THE HOME.

THIS "DIRT SACK HOUSE" IN EAST AUSTIN WAS A STOP ON THE 2014 WEIRD HOMES TOUR. IT IS MADE OF SACKS OF DIRT

IRA POOLE'S YARD IN THE 2400 BLOCK OF EAST MLK HAS ENTERTAINED DRIVERS FOR DECADES. THE METICULOUSLY MAINTAINED YARD'S FEATURES INCLUDE THE STATUE OF LIBERTY, A SPHINX, A MAP OF THE US, PAINTED TREE TRUNKS, AND MORE.

THIS JUXTAPOSITION OF INSTITUTIONS IN SOUTH AUSTIN SHOWS THE LIVE-AND-LET-LIVE ATTITUDE NECESSARY FOR THE GROWTH OF TRUE WEIRDNESS.

IT'S A TRIBUTE TO AUSTIN'S UNSERIOUSNESS THAT IT WOULD BUILD A HILL NEAR DOWNTOWN, THEN NAME IT AFTER AN ADOPTED SON FAMOUS FOR HIS COUNTRY-CONJUNTO-ROCK AND HIS DRUG CONSUMPTION. DOUG SAHM'S GHOST NOW GAZES UPON THE LARGIFICATION OF AUSTIN'S DOWNTOWN.

GENERALLY CONSIDERED THE JEWEL IN AUSTIN'S CROWN IS BARTON SPRINGS POOL. AT 900 FEET LONG AND A CONSTANT 68 DEGREES OF SPRING WATER, IT'S UNIQUE. OVER 800,000 PEOPLE VISIT ANNUALLY SO IT WAS A CHORE TO ASK EVERYONE TO LEAVE TO GET THIS SERENE PHOTO.

SMUT PUTT HEAVEN

Smut Putt Heaven comes from the fevered dreams of the amiable Scott Stevens. In South Austin, this homage to who-knows-what (actually Alice Cooper is a major influence) makes a visitor laugh nervously. The combination of rotting mannequin heads, crutches, golf clubs, and bottle-cap tree ornaments are not your everyday patio décor, and thank god. Scott started this artwork in 1995. The name "Smut Putt" comes from a comic book he created as a kid (he's a very talented cartoonist). "Heaven" was added to tie into the nearby Cathedral of Junk (see page 13). See more on Scott's handiwork at scottstevensart.com/links.html.

SCOTT STEVENS, THE "YARDIST" WHO CREATED SMUT PUTT HEAVEN.

I MADE THIS WHILE YOU WERE WATCHING TELEVISION

SMUT PUTT HEAVEN. WELCOME TO SCOTT'S NIGHTMARE.

IF GOOD FENCES MAKE GOOD NEIGHBORS, SCOTT IS THE BEST NEIGHBOR EVER.

SOUTH AUSTIN POPULAR CULTURE CENTER

South Austin Popular Culture Center, or South Pop, is dedicated to preserving the less hoity-toity aspects of Austin's culture, primarily music-related. A long wall memorializes deceased Austin-centric musicians and features revolving displays of posters and other artwork, often from the dean of local music illustration, Jim Franklin. It shares a space with the smoking accessory store Planet K. 1516-B S. Lamar Blvd., southpop.org.

SOUTHPOP FEATURES THIS LOVELY PARADE AROUND BACK.

Freddie King

Mambo' John Treanor

Stevie Ray Vaughan

THE GENIAL HENRY GONZALEZ IS THE FACILITY MANAGER AND AN ARTIST. IF YOU SEE HIM, ASK HIM TO EXPLAIN IT ALL.

TEXAS STATE CEMETERY

A surprisingly entertaining spot is the Texas State Cemetery in East Austin. In addition to hundreds of Civil War veterans, there are dozens of newer burial sites of notable Texans, all in a lovely park setting. The range of celebs is impressive, from Stephen F. Austin to Tom Landry to Ann Richards and J. Frank Dobie. 909 Navasota, cemetery.state.tx.us.

THE STATE CEMETERY HAS THIS ENIGMATIC COMMENTARY ON OUR SPECIES' FUTURE.

PA AND MA FERGUSON, THE ONLY HUSBAND-AND-WIFE GOVERNORS, DURING THE NINETEEN TEENS AND TWENTIES, SPIN SIDE BY SIDE, APPALLED AT THE CURRENT MEASLY CORRUPTION COMPARED TO THEIR HEYDAY.

THE MUSEUM OF NATURAL & ARTIFICIAL EPHEMERATA

The Museum of Natural and Artificial Ephemerata, "where you have been all along," is the handiwork of Scott Webel and Jen Hirt. They uncovered boxes of strange artifacts in Scott's grandfather's attic and have added to it over the years. The small facility in East Austin contains a surprising amount of high-quality oddities. The charming couple give tours, usually by appointment on Saturdays for a $5 donation. Watch their excellent website for special shows and events. 1808 Singleton Ave., mnae.org.

JEN HIRT AND SCOTT WEBEL WITH THEIR KIDS AMID THE WONDERS OF THEIR MUSEUM OF EPHEMERATA.

A LOCK OF ELVIS'S HAIR, CIGARETTE BUTTS FROM MARILYN MONROE, AND MAO TSE-TUNG'S ACUPUNCTURE KIT ARE JUST A SAMPLE OF THE PHANTASMAGORIA AT THE MUSEUM OF EPHEMERATA.

BEST Tribute to the Fleeting Museum of Natural and Artificial Ephemerata

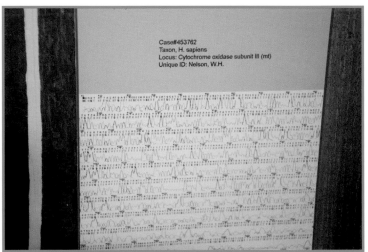

Case#453762
Taxon, H. sapiens
Locus: Cytochrome oxidase subunit III (mt)
Unique ID: Nelson, W.H.

A FANTASTIC NEW ADDITION TO THE COLLECTION IS THIS STRAND OF WILLIE NELSON'S HAIR (NOTE STRAND ON WHITE STRIP), WHICH THE CURATORS HAD ANALYZED. WILLIE'S GENOME IS DISPLAYED.

MOONLIGHT TOWERS

Austin is the only town in the world with Moonlight Towers. These nineteenth-century 165-feet tall urban lights were erected in 1895, bought secondhand from Detroit. There are seventeen of the original thirty-one left in the central Austin area. One serves as the base of the city's Zilker Park Christmas tree, with lights hanging down like a maypole. According to Ripley's Believe It or Not, in 1930, little Jimmie Fowler survived a fall from the top of a tower, bouncing down the interior shaft. This event is now re-created every year as part of the X Games.

A MOONLIGHT TOWER.

CHAPTER 2
WEIRD PEOPLE

AUSTIN'S WEIRDNESS COMES DOWN TO THE LARGE AND VARIED EVERYDAY FOLKS WHO ARE A BIT NONNORMAL AND WHO ARE REWARDED FOR IT. THIS TATTOOED LADY AND THIS CREATIVE PANHANDLER ARE BUT RANDOM SAMPLES.

Austin's weirdness ultimately comes from individual oddballs. Some are famous and extravagant—Crazy Carl Hickerson, for example (and of course, the late lamented Leslie Cochran)—but most are everyday eccentrics: a paramedic who hoards potatoes shaped like presidents, the guy who collects aluminum cans out of your recycling who has a PhD in philology, the city council candidate who can prove that cell phones are manifestations of extraterrestrial visitors. I often think how such people are celebrated in Austin but are scorned in most Texas towns.

It is these weirdos who are the bricks and mortar of our odd town. This is but a sample.

CARL HICKERSON

Carl Hickerson has been strutting his weirdness in Austin since the 1960s, when he started selling flowers on the Drag, attracting attention by deftly spinning a chrysanthemum on a finger, something he still does over forty years later, regularly, in front of Esther's Pool on 6th Street. He also dives into a kiddie pool wearing a bikini and flashes his self-induced "man boobs."

Carl gained further notoriety at Austin's Aquafest in the '70s when, to protest the speedboat races on (then) Town Lake that were a noise fest for East Austin, he swam out to the middle and cut the wires for the races' signals. He ran for Austin City Council eight times and mayor twice.

Carl is still a weirdo-about-town, almost always with his longtime companion, the incredibly patient and nice Charlotte Ferris. He can still put on a show, thank god. You should watch the documentary *Crazy Carl and His Man-Boobs*. Google that title to see a two-minute trailer for it.

CRAZY CARL HICKERSON DEMONSTRATES HIS TRADEMARK FLOWER-BALANCING SKILL AT A SCREENING OF THE DOCUMENTARY *CRAZY CARL AND HIS MAN-BOOBS*. HIS LONGTIME PARTNER CHARLOTTE FERRIS, AMONG OTHERS, LOOKS ON.

DR. DUMPSTER, A.K.A. DR. JEFF WILSON

Dr. Dumpster, a.k.a. Dr. Jeff Wilson, dean and associate professor of biological sciences at Huston-Tillotson University, is a perfect example of what Keep Austin Weird means: a smart, goofy, nice person who used the absurdity of living in a small Dumpster to make a point about materialism and sustainability. He started inhabiting the thirty-three square-foot Dumpster on campus in February 2014 and slowly made improvements over the months, until by February 2015, when he moved out, there was air conditioning, a "closet" (a false floor that opened), and a weather station. The Dumpster will continue as a teaching exhibit. He fostered an active environmental awareness organization at the historically African-American university called Black Is the New Green.

The anecdote that really amuses me about Dr. Dumpster is that when I was introduced to him as the guy who came up with Keep Austin Weird he was very interested and sincerely asked me if I thought what he was doing was weird! Wow, a college professor wonders if living in a Dumpster for over a year is weird. His standards for oddity are way up there.

The details of this noble effort may be followed at dumpsterproject.org.

As of 2015, he has started a new project to go for 100 days sleeping at a different person's house each night, making a point of visiting the high and mighty and the low and gritty.

THE DUMPSTER PROJECT LED TO THE CREATION OF A STUDENT ORGANIZATION, GREEN IS THE NEW BLACK, AT THE HISTORICALLY AFRICAN-AMERICAN HUSTON-TILLOTSON UNIVERSITY. HERE STUDENTS FROM ALL OVER TOWN GATHERED FOR A TOUR AND DISCUSSION OF SUSTAINABILITY.

THE GOOD DOCTOR SHOWS THE CLOSET, ONE OF THE CLEVER ADAPTATIONS THAT HIS DUMPSTER GAINED OVER THE YEAR.

DR. MICHAEL MULLEN

Dr. Michael Mullen, the Visiting Vet, is a one-of-a-kind pet doctor. He doesn't look the part or talk the part we're supposed to expect from a medical professional. He only does house calls and frequently recommends little or no treatment, explaining that a lot of the advice normally given by vets is just to make money or cover one's ass. He'll clearly explain the science behind the situation and treatment if you want to hear it. He's great with handling the pets and the owners. It's a telling indicator of his personality that he recently won a liar's contest in Alabama, describing his coon hound's ability to herd raccoons.

DR. MICHAEL MULLEN, THE VISITING VET, IS AN UNLIKELY MEDICAL PRO AND MORE FUN THAN YOU'VE HAD WITH YOUR VET.

GINNY AGNEW & NANCY TOELLE

Starting around 2010, Ginny Agnew and Nancy Toelle have offered Free Advice on the north shore of Lady Bird Lake, near the kayak rentals. These two wise women tackle everything from the lovelorn to mystics and from lost souls to wisenheimers. If it's a sunny, warm Sunday, there's a good chance they'll be there, so spin 'em a good yarn and be repaid with sagacity galore. One of those under-the-radar activities that are the real heart of weirdness.

SUNDAY AFTERNOONS AT LADY BIRD LAKE OFTEN MEAN FREE ADVICE FROM THE SOLOMONIC GINNY AGNEW AND NANCY TOELLE.

BEN SARGENT

Ben Sargent, our town's Pulitzer Prize–winning editorial cartoonist for the *Austin American-Statesman* (now retired), has a fetish for trains and the past. He is a founder of the Austin Steam Train Association, and he serves as a conductor dressed in full authentic costume. His home has a wonderful room with an elaborate miniature train set with detailed scenery, plus his 1905 letterpress and tray after tray of type for his handset printing business. The room is a most pleasant time machine. His cartoons are beautifully rendered and dead on target. He continues to cartoon for the *Texas Observer*. See his different skills on display at www.austinsteamtrain.org and texasobserver.org/author/ben-sargent.

BEN SARGENT POINTS TO THE PULITZER PRIZE HE WON FOR HIS EDITORIAL CARTOONS.

A 1905 LETTERPRESS SUITS BEN SARGENT'S WORLDVIEW PERFECTLY.

SARGENT PLAYS GULLIVER IN HIS MINIATURE TRAIN WORLD.

JOHN KELSO

John Kelso has highlighted Austin's—and humankind's— weirdness, both good and bad, in the *Austin American-Statesman* since 1977, a remarkable feat in the topsy-turvy world of print journalism. In 2014 he semi-retired to a once-a-week column from his previous thrice. One of his specialties is skewering pompous and self-satisfied folks, frequently the largely Republican state officials, which goes over well in liberal Austin, but not so good in that granite dome in the center of town. His dislike of the Dallas Cowboys, however, brought him his most vicious responses. He also highlights ordinary folks, such as cranky bartenders and good ol' boys who've met Bigfoot and the ongoing demise of smaller Austin's funkiness. He has written several books, including *Texas Curiosities: Quirky Characters, Roadside Oddities & Other Offbeat Stuff*.

JOHN KELSO IS THE LONGTIME CHRONICLER OF AUSTIN'S OFF-KILTER SIDE.

VIC AYAD

Vic Ayad, a refugee of Amarillo, is in a certain way, the oddest of the characters covered here. He's a very wealthy commercial real estate investor, one of the principals of Castle Hill Partners, which owns the beautiful castle overlooking the HOPE Outdoor Gallery (see Weird Art, page 48, for more). This building from 1869 was originally the Texas Military Institute. It went through many uses but by the early 2000s, was a mess, occupied by vagrants and filled with debris. Vic and partners rescued it and today it's spectacular, beautifully restored, and filled with antiques.

I met Vic late one evening in the Clarksville neighborhood. My wife was walking our dog and saw a man pull up to the Fresh Plus Grocery in a 1940 perfectly restored Mercury convertible. She told him that her husband would love it and rushed home to get me. Vic was very gracious and overly "impressed" that I was the idiot who came up with Keep Austin Weird. He gave me a 100-yard ride back to my house, and we exchanged email addresses. Our first lunch included Chris Layton, the drummer for the legendary Double Trouble—Stevie Ray Vaughan's band—who is a longtime friend of Vic's. That day Vic was driving a gorgeous '50s Studebaker. I asked him how many classic cars he owned. "Only six, but I do have thirty-one vintage motorcycles,

too." Turns out he collects all sorts of things related to popular music, including five of James Brown's capes. He had recently bought many items at an auction of the Armadillo World Headquarters's owner, Eddie Wilson, most notably Jim Franklin's huge painting of an armadillo bursting out of Freddie King's chest.

Vic's office is in the top of the tower of the castle overlooking the graffiti park and with a spectacular view of downtown. I was taken aback when I walked in to see a couple of automatic weapons on the sofa. Vic saw my reaction and laughed. "Those are paintball guns. Sometimes I have to go down and edit the graffiti." The top of the HOPE Outdoor Gallery has a fifty-foot-wide cement area that's right below his office. It's the scene for all sorts of gatherings. Vic's favorite is nude yoga.

VIC AYAD, RIGHT, IS THE PATRON OF THE HOPE OUTDOOR GALLERY. HIS GOOD PAL IS CHRIS LAYTON, DRUMMER OF DOUBLE TROUBLE.

PENNY VAN HORN

Penny Van Horn, a longtime personal friend, represents a happily large vein of eccentric ore that runs through Austin—mother, homeowner, state worker, crazy as a loon. Penny is a talented artist (her illustrations appear in this book). She has collections of cat whiskers and mosquitoes she has dispatched and pieces of wood chewed by gerbils. You know, the usual.

PENNY VAN HORN IS YOUR RUN-OF-THE-MILL TOTALLY LOONY AUSTINITE. HERE SHE HOLDS HER COLLECTION OF MOUNTED CAT WHISKERS AND NEARBY IS ONE OF THE DONORS. SEVERAL OF HER ILLUSTRATIONS DECORATE THIS VOLUME.

STEFANIE DISTEFANO

Stefanie Distefano is an artist who specializes in public works using mosaics, ranging from Gandhi at a convenience store to decorating entire bridges. She oversaw the production of the Larry Monroe Forever Bridge at Stacy Park in 2015, honoring the late popular DJ, but before that she decorated a small bridge just outside her own house in South Austin. Despite the beauty of it, the city objected just because that's what they do. A lawyer with contacts in high places convinced officials to back off, stating the obvious—that this sort of stuff is what makes our city special. Amazingly, this time they got it. Stefanie is relentlessly creative. Her home is the inside of a kaleidoscope.

STEFANIE DISTEFANO IN HER HOME, WHICH IS A PERFECT REFLECTION OF HER.

THE MAHATMA AT AN EAST AUSTIN CONVENIENCE STORE.

THE BRIDGE OUTSIDE STEFANIE'S HOME THAT CAUSED TROUBLED WATERS WITH THE CITY.

THE LARRY MONROE FOREVER BRIDGE, HONORING A BELOVED RADIO PERSONALITY.

MATTHEW McCONAUGHEY

CHAPTER 3
WEIRD ART

THE HOPE OUTDOOR GALLERY

The city's decision to add dopamine to the water supply a few years ago seemingly led to the explosion of public murals in Austin. The HOPE Outdoor Gallery is the apotheosis of this, but evidence is everywhere. It's perhaps the best overall trend in Austin and fights that nagging feeling that weird is fading like a 1998 Ramones T-shirt.

THE HOPE OUTDOOR GALLERY SITS WITH SARCASTIC MAJESTY IN OLD WEST AUSTIN.

I WAS PHOTOGRAPHING WHEN THIS NICE YOUNG WOMAN HAPPENED BY AND I ASKED IF SHE'D MIND POSING FOR A PHOTO FOR THIS BOOK. IT TURNED OUT SHE AND HER BOYFRIEND HAD ARRIVED A COUPLE OF HOURS EARLIER FROM FRANCE. THEY HAD SPECIFICALLY COME TO TOWN BECAUSE OF THE PHRASE KEEP AUSTIN WEIRD AND BOUGHT T-SHIRTS AT THE AIRPORT. THEY PRETENDED TO BELIEVE ME WHEN I TOLD THEM I INVENTED THE PHRASE.

THE SECRET AUSTIN WORLD GOVERNMENT'S PROPAGANDA MACHINE MUST HAVE DONE THIS ONE.

NOW WE KNOW WHERE PICASSO GOT HIS IDEAS.

THE ARTISTS' PALETTE.

THE HOPE OUTDOOR GALLERY IS, LIKE THIS IMAGE, A DREAMSCAPE.

MORE MURALS

This slice of heaven is in the 1100 block of Baylor Street in Old West Austin. This site was a condo project started in the '80s but abandoned due to geological problems. Giant cement slabs were left, and soon graffiti naturally appeared, but it generally was boring amateurish tags. But in March 2011 it took on its new name (although most just call it the graffiti park), founded by famed street artist Shepard Fairey and a couple of locals, notably Vic Aday (see page 42 in the Weird People chapter), who owns the land, including the Castle that looms above the scene, and Andi Scull Chetham, who more or less created the gallery from a seedy mess. With Fairey initiating the new graffiti, they invited artists to decorate the slabs. It has exploded into a very lively, constantly changing urban mural. A particularly cool event was during SXSW in 2012. The neighborhood was bummed because one day all the walls were painted gray. But that all radically changed when a few dozen artists showed up en masse. Free beer and DJs made it an all-day party at the end of which the walls were again alive. A book chronicling the park was published in 2014: *The HOPE Outdoor Gallery Book: 3 Years of Stories, People and Street Art in Austin, Texas*.

How long the do-gooder supporters are willing and able to pay the substantial property taxes is a daunting question. Here's hoping. 1101 Baylor St., hopecampaign.org/hopeprojects/hope-outdoor-gallery.

Shown here are other examples of Austin murals from around town.

TWO EAST AUSTIN TREASURES.

ONE OF THE NOUVEAU ICONIC ICONS ON THE EAST SIDE OF TOWN.

SADLY THIS TRIBUTE TO GENETIC ENGINEERING DISAPPEARED IN 2015.

THIS HYDE PARK BEAUTY IS A TRIBUTE TO THE UPCOMING GENRE WAR AMONGST CARTOONISTS.

THE EYES OF ARTISTS ARE UPON YOU AT JERRY'S ARTARAMA.

IT'S A HARD-FOUGHT WAR AS TO WHICH OF THESE HAS APPEARED IN THE MOST SELFIES: ROADHOUSE RELICS VS. JO'S COFFEE VS. HI, HOW ARE YOU (WHICH IS ON THE SIDE OF THE WONDERFULLY NAMED RESTAURANT THAI, HOW ARE YOU).

THIS 120-FOOT MOSAIC MURAL IN THE SWELL NORTH AUSTIN CRESTVIEW NEIGHBORHOOD WAS DESIGNED BY THE LOCALS AND EXECUTED BY ARTIST JEAN GRAHAM. 7100 WOODROW AVE.

EAST AUSTIN STUDIO TOUR

The East Austin Studio Tour (EAST) is a monster in a beret. This showcase of fine artists (compound noun, not an opinion), begun in 2001, has steadily grown to two fall weekends and to well over 400 studios, galleries, and pop-up garrets, proof of what a giant herd of dabblers and dab hands now roams free in town. And these folks must breed like cockroaches because there are now studio tours for West Austin, Travis Heights, and more. But EAST is the biggie and has become so well attended that it harkens to Yogi Berra's line, "No one goes there anymore; it's too crowded."

EAST is arguably the most accurate barometer of how East Austin has transformed since the turn of the century from a funky ethnic village feel, to hipster central, for good and ill. For instance, the Canopy, a hive of studios and galleries and shoppes and chai-erias, is on the site of the former Goodwill last-call store, where the junk that didn't sell at the others was piled up and dug through, in a fun third-world atmosphere. A loss or a gain? See east.bigmedium.org.

THE WACKY BLUE GENIE STUDIO WAS PART OF THE EAST AUSTIN STUDIO TOUR AND INCLUDED BUILD-YOUR-OWN MODEL CAR RACES DOWN THE LONG TRACK. (THE LOVELY WOMAN IS MY WIFE. LUCKY MAN.)

A TYPICAL EAST GALLERY VISITOR TRIES TO CHAT UP AN ARTWORK.

HELLO LAMP POST AUSTIN

This municipally funded project let smartphone users exchange text messages with statues, trees, libraries, swimming pools, etc. Based on an idea pioneered in other cities, beginning in February 2015, about twenty pieces of "street furniture" participated. Read more at hellolamppostaustin.com.

ONE STOP ON THE TEXTING TOUR HELLO LAMP POST. THIS ONE FEATURED A DEPRESSING INTERACTION WITH TREATY OAK, THE 500-YEAR-OLD SACRED INDIAN TREE THAT BARELY SURVIVED AN ASSASSINATION ATTEMPT IN 1989 BY AN ASS WHO WAS TRYING TO IMPRESS A WOMAN. THE OAK TEXTED OF ITS POST-TRAUMATIC STRESS AND INSATIABLE DESIRE FOR MULCH. SAD.

FORKLIFT DANCEWORKS

About once a year Austin is blessed with a new production of off-kilter choreography from Alison Ore and musician Graham Reynolds. Forklift became famous with "Trash Dance" in 2009 that featured city sanitation workers and their equipment in choreographed movements on the runway of the old airport. Since then they have produced a similar project with the Austin Energy electrical workers climbing telephone poles and gracefully maneuvering bucket cranes in synch. The year 2015 saw the city Urban Forestry employees caring for the city parks' trees moving to the original music of Reynolds. See a roundup of past and upcoming projects at forkliftdanceworks.org.

THE CITY'S URBAN FORESTRY WORKERS PERFORMING "THE TREES OF GOVALLE," ONE OF FORKLIFT DANCEWORKS TRIBUTES TO THE GRACEFULNESS OF MANUAL LABORERS.

MONOCHROME FOR AUSTIN

More than seventy canoes mysteriously crashed at the corner of 26th and Speedway on the University of Texas campus in the spring of 2015. *Monochrome for Austin* by sculptor Nancy Rubins is a wonderful addition to that bland, overcrowded part of campus. It stands over fifty feet tall and also stands for the importance of silliness.

CANOE PILE-UP ON THE UT CAMPUS.

ALISON ORR, THE ARTISTIC DIRECTOR AND CHOREOGRAPHER FOR FORKLIFT.

ESTHER'S FOLLIES

A stalwart champion of Austin's quirky side, Esther's has been going—hard to believe—since 1977, the same year as the first *Star Wars* movie (which is actually the sixth, or something). Founded and still run by Shannon Sedwick and Michael Shelton, this blend of vaudeville, stand-up, magic, skits, satire, and outside agitators is a core part of East 6th Street's reputation as one of the nation's foremost entertainment districts.

The building at Red River and E. 6th is now iconic, with its lovely murals, but it is the fourth location. The innovative design, with large windows directly behind the stage, allows outside performers and passing weirdos to be part of the show. The meister of these is Crazy Carl Hickerson (see page 37 in the Weird People chapter).

Shannon Sedwick, the driving force as both producer and performer, is a longtime friend of the author, having known each other since the third grade and serving on our high-school yearbook staff together. She and her husband, Michael Shelton, met as undergrads at UT appearing in avant garde plays and should be made official royalty of Austin. Shannon has served for many years as the president of the Old Pecan Street Association, which has done much to keep this unruly street just ruly enough to soldier on. Their latest activity is to install plaques honoring people and places from the street's gaudy history. 581 E. 6th St., esthersfollies.com.

SHANNON SEDWICK, COFOUNDER AND PERFORMER IN ESTHER'S FOLLIES, OUTSIDE THE BEMURALED THEATER.

SHANNON REHEARSES HER FAMOUS ACROBATIC ROUTINE.

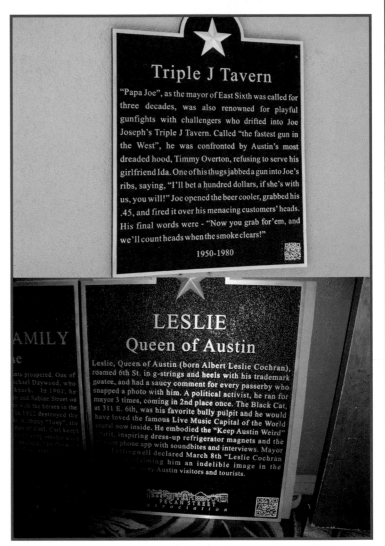

Triple J Tavern

"Papa Joe", as the mayor of East Sixth was called for three decades, was also renowned for playful gunfights with challengers who drifted into Joe Joseph's Triple J Tavern. Called "the fastest gun in the West", he was confronted by Austin's most dreaded hood, Timmy Overton, refusing to serve his girlfriend Ida. One of his thugs jabbed a gun into Joe's ribs, saying, "I'll bet a hundred dollars, if she's with us, you will!" Joe opened the beer cooler, grabbed his .45, and fired it over his menacing customers' heads. His final words were – "Now you grab for'em, and we'll count heads when the smoke clears!"

1950-1980

LESLIE
Queen of Austin

Leslie, Queen of Austin (born Albert Leslie Cochran), roamed 6th St. in g-strings and heels with his trademark goatee, and had a saucy comment for every passerby who snapped a photo with him. A political activist, he ran for mayor 3 times, coming in 2nd place once. The Black Cat, at 311 E. 6th, was his favorite bully pulpit and he would have loved the famous Live Music Capital of the World mural now inside. He embodied the "Keep Austin Weird" spirit, inspiring dress-up refrigerator magnets and the phone app with soundbites and interviews. Mayor Leffingwell declared March 8th "Leslie Cochran claiming him an indelible image in the Austin visitors and tourists.

UNDER SHANNON'S LEADERSHIP, THE OLD PECAN STREET ASSOCIATION IS PUTTING UP PLAQUES TO COMMEMORATE DIRTY SIXTH'S COLORFUL PAST. THE TRIPLE J PLAQUE IS ON THE SIDE OF THE CURRENT ESTHER'S. THE ONE HONORING THE LATE LESLIE COCHRAN AWAITS ITS PLACE.

CAPITAL AREA STATUES

A group of Austin big thinkers began in the '90s to install highly crafted bronzes commemorating iconic local people. Pulitzer Prize winner Lawrence Wright, musician Marcia Ball, writer Stephen Harrigan, and others formed Capital Area Sculptures and are responsible for three installations so far: The Philosophers' Rock by Barton Springs Pool, where '50s smarty pants J. Frank Dobie, Roy Bedichek, and Walter Prescott Webb frequently met to discuss matters philosophical; Angelina Eberly, the woman who fired a cannon on Congress Avenue to alert folks that Sam Houston was stealing the state archives in an attempt to move the capitol to his eponymous-ville; and the latest, Willie Nelson, located on the stretch of West 2nd Street renamed Willie Nelson Boulevard. The opening ceremony for it was held in 2012 on April 20 at 4:20 PM (for you L7s, that's all secret code). See page 117 and page 68 for images of the latter two sculptures.

THE PHILOSOPHERS' ROCK AT BARTON SPRINGS POOL, THE FIRST OF CAPITAL AREA SCULPTURES'S INSTALLATIONS, CELEBRATES SMART OLD MEN.

STEVIE RAY VAUGHAN STATUE

Famed professional golfer Vaughan, who once had a hole-in-one on the tricky alligator dual-level hole at Peter Pan Mini Golf, tragically drowned during a snow-cone crawl midday in August 1990. This statue by Lady Bird Lake shows him with his patented oversized putter. None of the buildings shown were there when he died.

SRV, THE FINEST PROFESSIONAL GOLFER AUSTIN HAS PRODUCED. FAMED FOR HIS PATENTED DOUBLE SHADOW.

MAKER FAIRE

Maker Faire is a celebration of DIY goofiness that periodically shows up in Austin. It features everything from quilting to robot wars. There are mini and maxi faires. Usually someone is flinging watermelons with a homemade trebuchet while nearby a glassblower sneezes a monster.

MAKER FAIRE BRINGS OUT AUSTIN BIKE ZOO CREATIONS AND ART CARS.

SCULPTURE

THE SOMEWHAT BLANDLY PLEASANT MUELLER AREA DOES HAVE THE EXCITEMENT OF GIANT RADIOACTIVE SPIDERS.

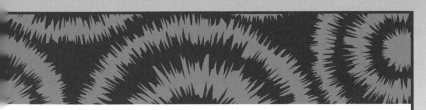

THIS WONDERFUL SCULPTURE ON SOUTH CONGRESS BY JAMES TALBOT (SEE WEIRD PLACES, PAGE 21, ON NEVERLANDIA) IS PART OF THE CITY'S ART IN PUBLIC PLACES.

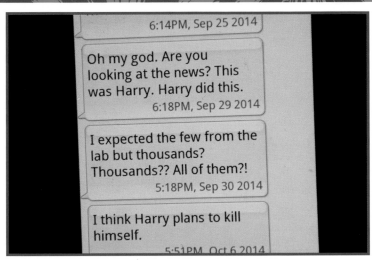

6:14PM, Sep 25 2014

Oh my god. Are you looking at the news? This was Harry. Harry did this.
6:18PM, Sep 29 2014

I expected the few from the lab but thousands? Thousands?? All of them?!
5:18PM, Sep 30 2014

I think Harry plans to kill himself.
5:51PM, Oct 6 2014

A PLAY TOTALLY DELIVERED BY ALMOST DAILY TEXT MESSAGES OVER SIX MONTHS WAS, UH, LENGTHY.

EVERYDAY YARD ART SUCH AS THIS ABOUNDS, ESPECIALLY IN EAST AUSTIN.

TYPEWRITER RODEO FEATURES LIVE POETS HAMMERING OUT QUALITY VERSE-ON-DEMAND USING MANUAL TYPEWRITERS.

CHAPTER 4
WEIRD MUSIC

"Live Music Capital of the World" is a trademarked official Austin motto, so it legally has to be true. With over 250 venues, a national TV series going since 1974, and two major and a dozen smaller festivals, the scene is flypaper for weirdoes with ears.

SOUTH BY SOUTHWEST

The first SXSW, in 1987, had 700 attendees; now there are 2,200 bands and over 35,000 attendees as the event has expanded into film and "interactive" (meaning digital), which is actually bigger than the music portion. There are also smaller .edu and eco sessions, stretching the entire event to two weeks. It has become a general party scene, with many coming just for free music and booze. Such events outnumber official ones now. It's a great time. The downtown atmosphere is buzzier than a Manhattan apartment intercom. Great people watching—if you like black clothes.

The money it brings in is phenomenal: downtown hotels at 100% capacity for nine straight days at double their usual rates; $46 million in alcohol sales for the period; 845% increase in aspirin sales. See sxsw.com.

AH, SXSW. EVERY CORNER DOWNTOWN HAS ITS QUOTA OF BLACKENED MUSICIANS WAITING FOR THEIR EIGHTH NONPAYING CORPORATE GIG.

THE TRUE ESSENCE OF SXSW IS OBSCURE BANDS PLAYING IN SMALL VENUES, SUCH AS THIS SHOWCASE AT THE LOVELY CAROUSEL LOUNGE.

AUSTIN CITY LIMITS AND ACL FEST

The *Austin City Limits* public TV show started in 1974 at local PBS station KLRN (now KLRU). In a choice that Jesus hisself couldn't improve on, Willie Nelson was on the opening show. It frequently struggled to stay on the air at various times in the '70s and '80s, but settled into the niche where it now is the longest running music program in television history and a member of the Rock & Roll Hall of Fame. It's relocation from the smallish studio with free beer on the UT campus to downtown next to the glitzy W Hotel complex may cause sighs among some senior fans, but it draws big crowds. The site was sanctified when a larger than life statue of Willie Nelson miraculously appeared in the plaza just outside. One of Austin's best institutions. See acltv.com.

In 2002, ACL Fest appeared in Zilker Park, with about 30,000 in attendance each day (currently 75,000 each for six days over two weekends). Mainly big-name groups, with some locals tossed in, make up the 130-plus band lineup. They've been plagued with 110 degree temperatures, floods, dust storms, and fires, which only seem to serve as fertilizer for its popularity. More at aclfestival.com.

NOT ALL SXSW MUSICIANS DRESS IN BLACK, AS THIS OUTLIER ILLUSTRATES.

IN 2012 ON APRIL 20 AT 4:20 PM THIS STATUE OF WILLIE NELSON MAGICALLY APPEARED IN A PUFF OF SMOKE JUST OUTSIDE THE AUSTIN CITY LIMITS VENUE. IT RESTS ON WILLIE NELSON BOULEVARD. COINCIDENCE?

FUNFUNFUN FEST

Many locals prefer this smaller event (begun 2006) as its big sibling festivals grow to unwieldy popularity. But even it has expanded to three days in the fall at Auditorium Shores, rather than the smaller Waterloo Park. Featured are indie groups—particularly metal and hip-hop—comedy, and sports, such as a mechanical bull riding. They always book at least one notably weird act, such as Weird Al Yankovich or Snoop Dogg.

REGGAE FESTIVAL

Begun in '93, when it was the Bob Marley Festival, Reggae Festival is a three-day celebration of uplifting music and herbs. It raises lots of money for the Capital Area Food Bank. In 2014 a guest drummer was Austin's not-so-favorite son, Lance Armstrong. Also the event happened in 2014 on April 20, a date that celebrates what reggae celebrates. More: austinreggaefest.com.

PACHANGA FEST

The name means "lively party" in Spanish, appropriate for this one-day event in May. All sorts of Latin-based music, traditional and edgy, is featured. NPR called it "Austin's Best-Kept Secret." It began at Auditorium Shores in 2008, but is now in East Austin's Fiesta Gardens. See pachangafest.com.

URBAN MUSIC FESTIVAL

Austin doesn't have a great reputation as an African-American sort of place, so this two-day festival has served a "serious" role in addressing that problem since 2005. It is held the same weekend as the Texas Relays, a large track-and-field event at UT that also draws a largely black crowd. Read about it at austinurbanmusicfestival.com.

OLD SETTLER'S MUSIC FESTIVAL

This actually is a captured moon of Austin, orbiting us but not quite in our grasp. It began in 1987 in nearby Round Rock and has moved to nearerby Driftwood. It goes for four days in the spring and many camp there so they can sleep off barbecue hangovers more easily. Americana and roots rock are the prevailing genres, neither of which would like the word "genre." Website: oldsettlersmusicfest.org.

VENUES

Trying to keep up with live music venues in this town is like trying to count the blades on a revolving fan. They come, they go, they change names. Here are some venerable stalwarts.

THE CONTINENTAL CLUB

The Continental Club on South Congress has been going since 1957. What originally was a classy nightspot (Glenn Miller's and Tommy Dorsey's bands played there) devolved into a strip joint in the '60s and '70s (Candy Barr disrobed there) then went even lower by going to its current incarnation as a roots rock dive (Stevie Ray Vaughan, Butthole Surfers, etc). The premier iconic rock live music venue that's still going. Check it out at www.continentalclub.com/Austin.html.

THE HOLE IN THE WALL

The Hole in the Wall is a friendly dive bar on "The Drag" part of Guadalupe, across from the university. This legendary venue has been going since 1974. Tall tales of late-night jams by famous rockers and drunken antics abound. In a city where slickness is increasingly celebrated, The Hole in the Wall has stuck to its double vision. The best sign they ever posted on their marquee described the place well: Cheap Music, Fast Drinks, Live Women. Read details of the debauchery at holeinthewallaustin.com.

THE LITTLE LONGHORN SALOON

Begun in the early '90s by Ginny Kalmbach, The Little Longhorn Saloon is a slice of honky-tonk perfection featuring live genuine country music—no Nashville bland—every night. It almost closed for good in 2013, when Ginny, then 78, decided to retire. Longtime performer there and star in his own right, Dale Watson bought the place, did some minimal renovations, and the joint's still jumping, filled with a swell mix of old-school folks and hipsters. Sunday afternoons bring the famed highlight: Chicken Shit Bingo, which started way back in 2002. A plywood grid with fifty-six numbers, which you can bet on for two dollars each, is the stage for a chicken to strut around until it selects the lucky number. The perfect place to take a first date; if they are appalled you get to keep shopping. 5434 Burnet Road, thelittlelonghornsaloon.com.

BLACK BEAUTY ENTHRALLS THE CROWD WITH HIS DEFECATORY SKILLS.

DALE WATSON, LEFT, NEW OWNER OF THE LITTLE LONGHORN SALOON, GREETS FANS OUTSIDE HIS VERY OWN HONKY TONK.

GINNY KALMBACH, FORMER OWNER OF THEN GINNY'S LITTLE LONGHORN, STILL SERVES AS OFFICIAL SPREADER OF THE FEED ON THE BINGO BOARD.

THE BROKEN SPOKE

Rolling along since 1964, The Broken Spoke features live music, very active two-stepping, and—most rare—an edible chicken-fried steak. Big acts from Bob Wills to Willie Nelson have performed there. It must be said, though, that this place is a prime example of the forces of "progress" impinging on weird Austin. In 2013, a $60 million housing conglomeration began surrounding it at close quarters. The previous, quaint dusty parking lot has morphed into something paved. The place nobly holds on, but it's ominous. It sort of looks like a quaint exhibit. 3201 S. Lamar, brokenspokeaustintx.com.

THE MINOR MISHAP MARCHING BAND IS A TRUE REPRESENTATIVE OF WEIRD AUSTIN.

CHAPTER 5

WEIRD GRUB & BOOZE

JUST HOW PATHETIC IT IS TO SPEND YOUR WHOLE LIFE IN CAFES AND CABARETS

GRUB

Austin has a growing reputation as a foodie town: there are lots of trendy new restaurants with shaved arugula sorbet for $12 and also more than 1,300 licensed food trucks serving everything from Korean-Martian fusion to old-school snow cones. Complex cocktails involving infusions of cash mixed with locally distilled eggplant liqueur plus approximately ten thousand small breweries have created a travel journalist's expense-account heaven. Here's a smorgasbord of Austin's weirder eateries and drinkeries.

THE UBIQUITOUS FOOD TRUCKS OFTEN GATHER TO PROTECT THEMSELVES FROM MARAUDING RESTAURANTS. HERE IN SOUTH AUSTIN THEY HAVE BANDED TOGETHER TO CELEBRATE NOTABLE AUSTIN WEIRDOS.

GOURDOUGH'S IS FAMOUS FOR THE DECADENCE OF THEIR DOUGHNUTS, E.G., THE FAT ELVIS: GRILLED BANANAS & BACON WITH PEANUT BUTTER ICING & HONEY. THEIR LATEST FLAVOR IS BRICK 'N' MORTAR AS THEY, LIKE SEVERAL OTHER TRAILERS, HAVE EXPANDED TO SIT-DOWN SITES.

THIS VERY DISTURBING FOOD TRUCK FROM AUSTIN PETS ALIVE SERVES MYSTERY DISHES LIKE MUTT ON RYE AND FILET OF FELIDAE.

FRANKLIN BARBECUE ROSE FROM FOOD-TRUCKDOM TO A NORMAL, IF FUNKY, RESTAURANT. IT IS GENERALLY REGARDED AS THE GREATEST BARBECUE IN THE GALAXY, AND THE QUEUE FOR 'CUE FOR ITS LIMITED LUNCH QUOTA IS SOME PEOPLE'S IDEA OF FUN. THE FIRST FOLKS IN LINE HERE ARRIVED AT 7:30 FOR THE 11:00 OPENING. 900 E. 11TH ST., FRANKLINBARBECUE. COM.

THERE MAY BE SOMETHING IN AUSTIN'S WATER (OR DOPE) THAT MAKES PEOPLE WANT TO WAIT IN LINE FOR FOOD. FRANKLIN BBQ IS THE WINNER, BUT HOPDODDY'S BURGERS IN SOCO HAS LONGER LINES THAN A MEDIEVAL POEM.

SAM'S BBQ IN EAST AUSTIN DOESN'T GET THE RESPECT IT DESERVES FOR ITS BRISKET, RIBS, AND SAUSAGE. IT'S A SUPERFUNKY DIVE WITH FRIENDLY FOLKS WHO'VE BEEN AT IT FOR DECADES. THE MANY SMOKED POSTERS ON THE WALLS SPEAK TO ITS HISTORY AS A MUSICIAN'S LATE-NIGHT HANGOUT (OPEN UNTIL 3:00 A.M. ON WEEKENDS). 2000 E. 12TH ST.

NUBIAN QUEEN LOLA'S CAJUN SOUL FOOD CAFÉ IS A UNIQUE TREASURE OF AUSTIN WITH EXCELLENT INEXPENSIVE HOMEMADE FOOD SERVED BY THE CHARMING QUEEN LOLA. MUCH OF HER EFFORTS AND MONEY GO TO FEEDING THE NEEDY, SO GO AND THROW IN A FEW EXTRA DOLLARS. 1815 ROSEWOOD AVE., NUBIANQUEENLOLA.COM.

QUEEN LOLA'S CAFÉ HAS THIS COMMUNITY CHAPEL IN THE BACK.

EVEN THE IRREDEEMABLY NORMAL FAST-FOOD PLACES HAVE SOME SENSE OF THE IMPORTANCE OF THINGS.

A FRANCHISE OPERATION THAT'S A BIT CUTESY WITH THEIR CADDY SHACK THEME, BUT THEY DO OFFER A MINIATURE GOLF COURSE IN BACK AS PART OF THE DEAL. THEY ALSO HAVE ALCOHOLIC MILK SHAKES. 7211 BURNET RD.

THE DEAN OF BURGER JOINTS AND STILL SERVING A DARN GOOD CHEESEBURGER AND EXCELLENT ONION RINGS IS DIRTY'S (AKA DIRTY MARTIN'S AND MARTIN'S KUM-BACK). THEY'VE BEEN CRANKING OUT THE CALORIES TO AN ENTERTAINING MIX OF STUDENTS, OLD TIMERS, HIPSTERS, AND NO-ACCOUNTS SINCE 1926. THE COMMON NAME STEMS FROM IT HAVING A DIRT FLOOR UNTIL 1951. IF YOU LIKE A SIDE OF TRADITION WITH YOUR FOOD, THIS IS THE PLACE. 2808 GUADALUPE, DIRTYMARTINS.COM.

MARIA'S TACO XPRESS IS A SOUTH AUSTIN STAPLE SINCE THE MID-1990S. IT, LIKE SO MUCH OF SOUTH LAMAR, HAS HAD TO FIGHT THE WAVES OF CONDOS AND MONEY THAT ARE TURNING A FORMERLY LOW-KEY SLIGHTLY REDNECK AREA INTO GENTRIFIED HOMOGENIZATION. HIPPIE CHURCH ON SUNDAYS FEATURES GOSPEL MUSIC WITH YOUR MIGAS. THE ICONIC FIGURE OF MARIA GUARDS ALL. 2529 S. LAMAR, TACOXPRESS.COM.

IN AUSTIN, ONE MUST PAY OBEISANCE TO THE HEALTHFUL GUARDS POSTED AT THE FOOD PYRAMID. PICTURED IS AN ITEM THAT IS EVERYTHING YOU WANT TO HATE ABOUT WHOLE FOODS. A NEW ENTRY IN THE INNOCENT-FOOD VS. GUILTY-FOOD FIGHT IS RABBIT FOOD GROCERY. WHEATSVILLE CO-OP CONTENDS THAT THE TOKYO THAT GODZILLA ATE WAS GLUTEN-FREE.

IN A LAND RIFE WITH NIFTY NONCHAIN COFFEE HOUSES, SPIDER HOUSE STILL STANDS OUT AS AN EXEMPLAR. ITS OUTDOOR PATIO, FILLED WITH INTERESTING DEBRIS, BOTH MATERIAL AND HUMAN, CAPTURES THE ESSENCE OF AUSTIN WEIRDNESS. SINCE ITS FOUNDING IN 1995, IT HAS SPREAD TO INCLUDE THE NEXT-DOOR SPIDER HOUSE BALLROOM, HOME TO LIVE MUSIC, AND THE VILLAGE, SEVERAL FOOD TRUCKS, AND, OF COURSE, A TATTOO PARLOR.

BOOZE

An interesting division exists in the types of weird bars in town: There are old-school honky tonks (see also Weird Music chapter, starting on page 66) and dive bars and then there are new hip joints (good name for a geriatric bar).

A REALLY, REALLY OLD-SCHOOL DRINKERY IS THE JOINED-AT-THE-HIP SCHOLZ GARTEN AND SAENGERRUNDE HALL. OPENED IN 1866, SCHOLZ GARTEN IS THE OLDEST OPERATING BUSINESS IN TEXAS. THE LARGE NUMBER OF GERMAN IMMIGRANTS NEEDED A BEER HALL. MANAGEMENT HAS CHANGED HANDS MULTIPLE TIMES, BUT SINCE 1908 IT HAS BEEN OWNED BY AUSTIN SAENGERRUNDE, A GERMAN-HERITAGE SINGING AND BOWLING SOCIETY (SEE ALSO WEIRD SPORTS, PAGE 108). ITS LOCATION HAS MADE SCHOLZ A STRANGE MELTING POT OF POLITICIANS—ESPECIALLY OF THE ENDANGERED LIBERAL TYPE—AND UT SPORTS FANS AND LAZY STUDENTS AND PROFESSORS. 1607 SAN JACINTO, SCHOLZGARTEN.COM.

DONN'S DEPOT IS AN OLD TRAIN STATION WITH A COUPLE OF TRAIN CARS GRAFTED ON. IT'S THE APOTHEOSIS OF SOME-THING, IT'S JUST HARD TO KNOW WHAT. PART COUNTRY HONKY TONK, PART SMOOTH JAZZ BAR, PART PARODY OF A SEMI-SLIMY LOUNGE. LIVE MUSIC EVERY NIGHT HAS BEEN GETTIN' THEM DEE-VORCÉES ON THE DANCE FLOOR SINCE 1972. A REALLY FUN PLACE. 1600 W. 5TH ST., DONNSDEPOT.COM.

THE CAROUSEL LOUNGE HAS MORPHED FROM A KITSCHY LOUNGE IN 1963 TO A KITSCHY LOUNGE. YAY FOR STASIS! ITS LOCATION IS ENOUGH OFF THE BEATEN PATH TO KEEP IT WEIRD. THE MUSIC RANGES FROM CROONERS TO PUNK, BUT THOSE SCARY CLOWN FACES ALWAYS HAUNT. 1110 E. 52ND ST., CAROUSELLOUNGE.NET.

JUST A SHORT STAGGER WEST OF DONN'S AND HOUSED IN AN EX-CHAIN-SAW SHARPENING SHOP AND DEDICATED TO THE GHOST OF JOHNNY CASH, THE MEAN-EYED CAT BAR SITS AMID BRAND NEW CONDOS LIKE A TURD IN A PUNCHBOWL. WISH THEM WELL. 1621 W. 5TH ST., THEMEANEYEDCAT.COM.

EXEMPLARS OF HIP NEW WEIRD BARS ARE DOZEN STREET AND THE EAST SIDE SHOWROOM. THE FORMER STRESSES ITS ARTISTIC SPIN ON A COCKTAIL LOUNGE WITH LOTS OF WORK BY STEFANIE DISTEFANO (SEE WEIRD PEOPLE, PAGE 44), SISTER OF ONE OF THE OWNERS. LIVE MUSIC PLUS AN OUTDOOR AREA WHERE DOGS ARE WELCOME. THE EAST SIDE SHOWROOM, IN THE UBERHIP EAST AUSTIN BAR DISTRICT, HAS AN AMUSING STEAMPUNK DÉCOR. WATCH SILENT MOVIES WHILE SNACKING ON FARM-TO-TABLE TIDBITS. RUBE GOLDBERG IS GETTING SOUSED AT THE NEXT TABLE. 1808 E. 12TH ST., DOZENSTREET.COM & 1100 E.6TH ST., EASTSIDESHOWROOM.COM.

EXERCISE YOUR LEGS AND ELBOW ON THE PUBCRAWLER. THIS GROUP-BICYCLE BAR IS ALWAYS FILLED WITH LAUGHING BOOZEHOUNDS WHEN IT PLOWS AROUND DOWNTOWN. SEE PUBCRAWLEROFAUSTIN.COM.

CHAPTER 6
WEIRD EVENTS

It's almost laughable how many events take place constantly in Austin beyond the obvious giant ones, such as SXSW (see Weird Music, page 67, for more on that), ACL, etc. Some are recurring, most are one-timers. Increasingly they are not at all weird, such as the Food + Wine Festival. Look at the calendar section of the weekly *Austin Chronicle* or the events section of Austin Culturemap (austin.culturemap.com/events) or myriad other sites and be amazed at the number of at least somewhat oddball happenings. A random Saturday in July had almost three dozen listed, ranging from a celebration of Nikola Tesla to the Austin Leather Social gay dance to the Rooster Teeth Expo online gaming hoopla.

A major, recent loss in this category is Spamarama. The death of that parody of cook-offs that featured bizarre uses of the potted meat is a sad and venal tale of corporate intrigue. Hormel, maker of Spam—ironically headquartered in Austin, Minnesota—acquired the rights to Spamarama and has forgotten to hold the event since 2007. The world's easiest boycott: Don't buy Spam.

The ones below are generally not focused just on music, although one doesn't hold a bris without live music in Austin.

EEYORE'S

With the death of Spamarama, the mantle of premier weird event in Austin is draped on the capable shoulders of Eeyore's Birthday Party, the spring shindig begun by the UT English department in 1963 in Eastwoods Park with a few dozen pipe-smoking elbow patches and a keg. Now it's a massive day-long, free bacchanalia in Pease Park, with a different kind of pipe smoking. As the day goes along, the place goes from being a celebration of a beloved kiddie lit animal to a celebration of the animal nature of people. Up to 20,000 stroll around wearing costumes, some of them imaginary. Drum circles can be heard but usually not seen, obscured by clouds of fragrant smoke. Usually in April. Read all about it at eeyores.org.

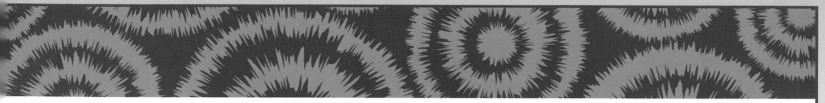

TYPICAL EEYORIANS.

ONE OF THE GREATEST TRIBUTES TO TESTOSTERONE EVER, A UNICYCLE FOOTBALL GAME AT EEYORE'S.

KEEP WACO WACKO

AN AMBASSADOR FROM A WEAKER LAND VISITS EEYORE'S TO OBSERVE AUSTIN'S SUPERIOR WEAPONRY.

CARNAVAL BRASILIERO

Since it's held in the chilly month of February, what's more natural than to wear as little as possible? This Lenten blowout (fun fact: "carnevale" means removal of meat...hmmm, perhaps a dig at the loss of Spamarama?) was begun in 1975 at the Austin Unitarian Church by a group of Brazilian students at UT. It's now one of the largest and craziest Brazilian carnivals outside that country. Just check Google Images to get a taste of the wanton nature of this bacchanal. The annual posters for it are collectors' items. See sambaparty.com.

KEEP AUSTIN WEIRD FEST & 5K

Begun in 2002 by the skunks who trademarked the phrase Keep Austin Weird for hats and shirts, this is now a worthy benefit for the Food Bank. The run is billed as the "slowest 5K on the planet" and participants are highly encouraged to sport costumes. Details: keepaustinweirdfest.com.

SADLY, THE NAMESAKE KEEP AUSTIN WEIRD EVENT IS ONE OF THE TAMER ONES ON THE ROTA. WHERE ARE THE KANGAROO LIMERICK CONTESTS AND LUMBER TASTINGS?

CAPITOL 10K

About the only genuinely odd things about this event are its longevity—it began in 1978—and size—16,000. A number of folks make the run a wee bit harder by wearing something stupid, and good for them. An admirable sense of priorities. In March, cap10k.com.

THE CAPITOL 10K IS ONE OF APPROXIMATELY 468 RUNS HELD IN TOWN. IT'S THE LARGEST IN TEXAS. DON'T THEY LOOK LIKE THEY'RE HAVING FUN?

HONK TX!

Honk TX! is an annual celebration of community bands from around the US, but they are not your staid Sousa musicians. These are nutso crews with unmatched enthusiasm. Honk is a multiday event, capped with a parade through East Austin. Austin's Minor Mishap Marching Band (see also Weird Music, page 73) is a stalwart at the event.

HONK TX! IS ONE OF THE HAPPIEST EVENTS YOU CAN ATTEND.

O. HENRY PUN-OFF

One Saturday every May, 9-1-1 is flooded with calls about deafening groans coming from downtown. But it's just the O. Henry Pun-Off World Championship, held since 1977. Named for the famed nineteenth-century Austin candy bar baron, dozens of punsters cross tongues in a cringe-inducing spittle fest. Get the scoop at punpunpun.com.

THESE ARE THE SCOREKEEPING DEVICES AT THE PUN-OFF.

REPUBLIC OF TEXAS RALLY

I reluctantly include this annual June tribute to noise and pollution, but the ROT Rally is the largest biker event in Texas. I guess it's weird to have tens of thousands of hairy, tattooed, bulky motorcyclists and their boyfriends all in one spot. Consider it a tribute to the accuracy of stereotypes. Go to rotrally.com.

BAT FEST

The pleasant days of August bring out the most intense nightly exodus of our 1.5 million Mexican free-tailed bats, the largest urban colony in the world. They slumber under the Ann Richards Congress Avenue Bridge until either their hunger for juicy mosquitoes or the live rock music from Bat Fest sends them out in clouds for the cheering masses. Bat Fest is a one-day salute to these amazing creatures' ability to sell souvenirs. Google the event for more info. For more scientific info on the bats, visit Bat Conservation International, batcon.org.

THIS IS A TRIBUTE TO OUR CITY'S NOCTURNAL EMISSION OF 1.5 MILLION TADARIDA BRASILIENSIS. NOTE WE CALL THEM MEXICAN FREE-TAILED BATS, BUT SCIENCE CALLS THEM BRAZILIAN. OUR GOVERNOR IS SENDING TROOPS TO THE BORDER TO SETTLE THIS.

DAY OF THE DEAD

Dia de Muertos, a solemn Mexican holiday to remember the deceased, is turned into a wacky excuse to drink and disguise oneself as a skeleton. Generally focusing on the Mexic-Arte Museum on Congress Avenue, there are parades, gigantes, and, of course, live music.

MEXI-CARTE MUSEUM'S CELEBRATION OF THE DAY OF THE DEAD ACCOUNTS FOR NINETY PERCENT OF THE CITY'S USE OF PAPIER-MÂCHÉ.

HALLOWEEN

Even more zombies than usual take over 6th Street for a stroll on Halloween every year, feasting on alcohol-soaked brains. It can be massive. Depending on the day of the week and the weather, up to 100,000 have been known to come howl and moon.

HIPSTERS VAINLY ATTEMPT TO DISGUISE THEMSELVES ON 6TH STREET ON HALLOWEEN.

HALLOWEEN ON 6TH STREET MEANS EVEN MORE BRAINLESSNESS THAN USUAL.

REAL AUSTINITES SCOFF AT TRADITIONAL JACK-O'-LANTERNS.

STAR OF TEXAS TATTOO REVIVAL

Since 2002, this paean to disfigurement has attracted ink-stained artistes from around the country. It's an odd scene: booth after booth of deeply concentrating needle-wielding weirdos hovering over partially dressed people in a variety of poses, depending on what appendage is getting decorated, the air buzzing with tattoo machines. Austin, as a leader in hipster culture, takes this very seriously.

THE STAR OF TEXAS TATTOO REVIVAL IS NOT MUCH DIFFERENT FROM MANY CONVENTIONS THAT MEET IN TOWN.

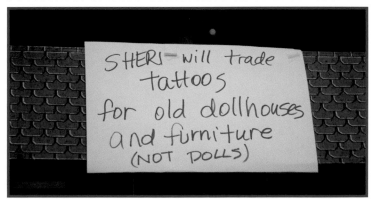

SHERI – will trade tattoos for old dollhouses and furniture (NOT DOLLS)

NOT THE USUAL SWAP 'N' SHOP.

ZILKER KITE FESTIVAL

Probably the longest running event in Austin, the Kite Festival began in 1929 as a metaphor for the stock market—flying high, crashing to earth. It's held the first Sunday in March, so it's always a crapshoot with the weather. In keeping with Austin's devotion to weirdness, one of the most-prized trophies is for "most unusual."

THE KITE FESTIVAL DEMONSTRATES THE CITY'S DEVOTION TO UNSERIOUSNESS AS IT HAS BEEN GOING SINCE 1929.

ARMADILLO CHRISTMAS BAZAAR

Typically, a sale of largely handmade items means a cringe-worthy collection of crude pastels of big-eyed kittens and needlepoints of deep thoughts, but the Armadillo has a high percentage of quality crafts from our area's deep tradition of artistes and hippie DIYers. The frosting on the snowman is the lineup of good live music (and not just Christmas carols). It's moved more times than the Cedar Door, but it has been going since 1975. See armadillobazaar.com.

MLK DAY PEACE THROUGH PIE

The Saturday before Martin Luther King Day is celebrated at the historic Sweethome Missionary Baptist Church—a lovely reminder of the Clarksville neighborhood's African-American origins—with gospel music, a reading of the I Have a Dream speech, and pie. Austin's Peace Through Pie organization participates in many events but the MLK Day peaceful pie fight is the oldest, begun in 2007. Visitors get to sample many pies and bid on dozens of others in a fundraiser for this venerable church. See them on Facebook by searching for Sweet Home Missionary Baptist Church.

SWEET HOME BAPTIST CHURCH HOSTS AN MLK DAY PEACE THROUGH PIE GALA EVERY YEAR.

WEIRD HOMES TOUR

Begun in 2014, this relative newcomer is evidence of the fighting spirit of Austin's weirdo-rights community. Their website in 2015 had this call to arms:

ACCORDING TO A 2014 ZANDAN POLL "NINE OUT OF 10 AUSTINITES THINK 'AUSTIN IS WEIRD' BUT OVER HALF SAY IT'S BECOMING MORE SIMILAR TO OTHER MAJOR US CITIES." WE WANT TO HIGHLIGHT THE MANY HOMES THAT ARE WORKING TO REVERSE THAT STATISTIC.

Eight homes were featured in the 2015 version, from Dr. Dumpster's humble abode (see Weird People, page 38) to Casa Neverlandia to the extravagant Johnson/Chronister mansion (see Weird Places, pages 21 and 25, for the latter two). Seriously unserious people doing God's work; view their site atweirdhomestour.com.

RUBE GOLDBERG CONTEST

Every February the engineering department at UT challenges its students with the Rube Goldberg contest, the challenge being to build the most overly complex machine possible to take twenty steps to perform some mundane task, such as erasing a blackboard. The students on the winning team are pretty much guaranteed jobs designing Ikea furniture.

UT ENGINEERING STUDENTS FIGHT FIERCELY TO COMPLEXIFY SIMPLE TASKS IN THE RUBE GOLDBERG CONTEST.

RODEO AUSTIN

This event is not normally thought of as weird, but it's always held the same time as SXSW, so the culture clash does spark.

CHRISTMAS DECORATIONS

Sadly one of the major Christmas weirdness highlights has become a shadow of itself. The joint blitz of lights the neighbors on W. 37th Street did for several years suffered when its ring-leader moved away. A few soldier on gamely, but the bloom is off the rose.

But another stalwart who carries on as strongly as ever is Willis Littlefield on W. 12th Street, in Clarksvillle. A man who decorates his home with a unique vision: angels, James Brown, pigs, many, many Santas, you name it. Every night he's out greeting folks and handing out candy canes. A couple of years ago a couple got married in the middle of it.

THIS STALWART ON WEST LYNN STREET HAS BEEN CONFUSING CHILDREN AT CHRISTMAS FOR YEARS.

WILLIS LITTLEFIELD HAS MASTERED CHRISTMAS DECORATIONS.

BIG JIM THEORY

And now let's go to Big Jim Theory at the sports desk. Hey, Big Jim, what's new in the wide, weird world of sports?

Howdy, folks. Well, we're in an odd period right now 'cause all Austin athletes have recently had existential crises when they realized sports are totally meaningless and they've wasted years of effort on something worthless. It all started when local hero Lance Armstrong was exposed as a fraud in 2012.

Then there followed years of mediocre—at best—UT football and basketball. The entire local big-time sports house of cards met a stiff breeze. An upside to this is that it put a positive spotlight on those sports that happily wallow in meaninglessness. So here's a cavalcade of local jocks and jockettes, doing their part to keep it weird.

MELLOW JOHNNY IS ARMSTRONG'S RETAIL STORE IN DOWNTOWN AUSTIN. THE NAME IS A PUN ON JELL-O AND MONEY, OR SOMETHING.

LOCAL BOY LANCE ARMSTRONG HAS INSPIRED MUCH HUMAN GROWTH . . . HORMONE-TAKING.

BOWLING

Guess which sport easily has the highest participation rate and the lowest TV ratings. Bowling! What other sport lets you drink during play while wearing rented shoes? Austin has two alleys that represent the edgy side.

Within the otherwise typical venue known as Dart Bowl is a world-class collection of bowling kitsch, displayed in multiple cases. (Your author must confess to his own such collection, so some bias is in play here.) And the café features really excellent enchiladas, albeit a bit on the greasy side. Get them with, incongruously, dinner rolls. Dee-lish. Be sure to thoroughly wash hands afterwards or you will drop your bowling ball and scuff your rented shoes. 5700 Grover, dartbowl.com.

A German singing society formed way back in 1852 and formally became the Saengerrunde in 1879. It is Austin's oldest ethnic organization. It began meeting at Scholz Garten complex (see Weird Grub and Booze, page 84, for more) in the 1860s, and there it remains. Along with singing and drinking beer, another German pastime was bowling and there is a nifty four-lane alley hidden away there (along with an emergency backup bar). 17th & San Jacinto, saengerrunde.org/bowling.html

DART BOWL HAS SEVERAL DISPLAY CASES OF HIGH-QUALITY BOWLING KITSCH AND AN EXCELLENT GREASY SPOON CAFÉ.

KEGS AND KEGLERS HAPPILY COEXIST AT THE ESOTERIC SAENGERRUNDE BOWLING ALLEY.

GOLF

Miniature golf has long held the title of official sport of weirdoes and Austin is blessed with a gem: Peter Pan Mini-Golf. Family-run since 1948, this thirty-six-hole layout—located on an incredibly valuable plot of land—has hosted several million birthday parties and first dates amid its cement menagerie. The owners had artist Cheryl Latimer refurbish the figures in 2011 so it's looking top-notch. It's even BYOB. 1207 Barton Springs, peterpanminigolf.com.

Right across the street, on even more valuable land, is Butler Pitch and Putt. This slice of heaven has been going since 1950. If you visit at the right time of year, you'll see fruit on the banana and pear trees while parrots squawk at your lame shots. How long these two beauties can hang on in central Austin is a canary in a minefield. 201 Lee Barton Dr., butlerparkpitchandputt.com.

PETER PAN MINI-GOLF IS OLD-SCHOOL WEIRDNESS NEWLY REFURBISHED.

FOOTGOLF

An unholy blend of soccer and golf has darkened the landscape. The Harvey Penick Golf Campus (gotta love the name), which has a real nine-hole golf course and focuses on training youth in the character-building properties of golf (swearing, drinking, lying), added footgolf in 2014. You don't need to have it explained, do you? 5501 Ed Bluestein Blvd., harvey-penickgc.com.

THE HARVEY PENICK GOLF CAMPUS OFFERS FOOTGOLF FOR THOSE TOO UNCOORDINATED TO PLAY REAL GOLF.

RUNNING

THE WEIRD EVENTS CHAPTER HAS MORE ON THE CORNUCOPIA OF RUNNING EVENTS, BUT THE KEEP AUSTIN WEIRD 5K BILLS ITSELF AS THE "SLOWEST 5K ON THE PLANET."

ROLLER DERBY

This sport's revival in 2001 began in Austin and spread to the rest of the planet. Austin has two leagues: Texas Rollergirls (flat track) and Texas Roller Derby (banked track), and they reportedly disdain the other. Fueled by live bands and cheap beer, the fans get to root for teams like the Texecutioners, Putas del Fuego, and the Hell Marys. Good, clean family fun.

BESIDES KEEPING AUSTIN WEIRD, THE ROLLERGIRLS KEEP IT CLEAN.

EXTREME SPORTS

Austin hit the big time in 2014 when ESPN's X Games selected Circuit of the Americas as its venue until at least 2017. Featuring crazed skateboarding, motocross, BMX, and other doctors' delights, it also has over-the-top foods. Deep-fried testosterone on a stick is a crowd fave.

But Austin's intrepid crazies don't need them big-city TV folks to do extreme sports. It's an everyday part of life, especially skateboarding at the House Park facility that opened in 2014.

THE X GAMES'S TWELVE-FLOOR SKATEBOARD DROP AT THE CIRCUIT OF THE AMERICAS DEFINED EXTREME.

THE ANTHILLS OF THE SAVANNAH. NEAR THE SKATE PARK, ON W. 9TH STREET, IS A HOMEMADE, BUT CITY-SANCTIONED BMX TRACK. WHEN EMPTY, IT LOOKS OTHERWORLDLY.

EVERYDAY AUSTIN HAS MORE THAN ITS SHARE OF EXTREME SPORTSPEOPLE. THE AUSTIN BMX AND SKATE PARK ON SHOAL CREEK OPENED IN 2011 AND IS GREAT PEOPLE-WATCHING, AS LONG AS THEY'RE NOT YOUR KIDS.

RACING

The Circuit of the Americas Formula 1 race has never seemed like a good fit for this city. Millionaire international jetsetters taking helicopter taxis just ain't Austin. But the venue does get a suitably weird event regularly: the Formula Sun Grand Prix, wherein university teams build solar vehicles for a grueling three-day marathon. The odd cars struggle to make it up the opening hill at the track, but then silently and gracefully glide around the course. Usually in sunny July. It's free, so if you're curious about COTA but are a cheapskate, here's your chance.

THE FORMULA SUN GRAND PRIX STARTS WITH A CHALLENGING CLIMB. THE SIMULTANEOUSLY SLEEK AND UNGAINLY CARS ARE BUILT BY UNIVERSITY STUDENTS.

PÉTANQUE

This French game is pronounced as if one were spitting out a bit of cork from a fine glass of Colombard. Fierce competitors throw metal balls at other metal balls while eating cheese and drinking fine *vins*. It is similar to bocce and boules. Austin's Heart of Texas Pétanque Club has wonderful informal matches every Wednesday and Sunday afternoons at the French Legation, the remnant of the only country besides the US to recognize the Republic of Texas. More at heartoftexas.wordpress.com.

THE BEST BIT OF SPORTS EQUIPMENT EVER—A RETRACTABLE MAGNET TO PICK UP PÉTANQUE BALLS.

THE MOST RECENT TIME I ATTENDED THE HEART OF TEXAS PÉTANQUE CLUB'S MATCHES AT THE FRENCH LEGATION, THERE WAS A FIFTEEN-MINUTE HEATED ARGUMENT OVER RULES THAT WAFTED BACK AND FORTH BETWEEN FRENCH AND ENGLISH.

CURLING

This sport (?) has gained well-deserved recognition during the winter Olympics as a goofy, addictive event, so it's appropriate that Austin has an active group, the Lone Star Curling Club. They meet Sunday mornings at Northcross Mall. It is more fun than church.

CURLING MAKES MINIATURE GOLF LOOK OVERLY SERIOUS.

CHAPTER 8
WEIRD POLITICS

WEIRD POLITICS

All politics is loco, said a great man. Austin has done its part both by hosting the bad-weird state legislators and breeding its own (mostly) good-weird local candidates.

From its very origins, Austin has been a political town. The tiny settlement of Waterloo was designated and designed in 1839 as the capital of the new Republic of Texas. In 1842 President Sam Houston, wanting to either protect the state archives from a Mexican invasion or steal them to move the capital to his eponymous metropolis, sent Rangers to get the papers. When they did the deed in the dark of night, a woman named Angelina Eberly fired a handy cannon (early example of open carry) at them. Alerted citizens rode after the Rangers and resecured the archives. Screw you, Houston.

Since then there has been a steady roster of local candidates and occasional actual elected goofballs. Here's a sampling of some notables:

THIS STATUE ON CONGRESS AVENUE MEMORIALIZES ANGELINA EBERLY'S ALERT THAT STARTED THE MULTI-HOUR ARCHIVES WAR.

• PERHAPS THE MOST FAMOUS WEIRDO CANDIDATE IN AUSTIN'S HISTORY WAS THE LATE, LAMENTED LESLIE COCHRANE. THIS BELOVED CROSS-DRESSING SEMIHOMELESS MAN AND WOMAN OF THE PEOPLE RAN FOR MAYOR OR CITY COUNCIL THREE TIMES, GARNERING UP TO EIGHT PERCENT OF THE VOTES.

• JOHN JOHNSON WAS A MAFIA HITMAN TURNED STOOLIE WHO WAS RELOCATED FROM NEW JERSEY TO AUSTIN IN THE WITNESS PROTECTION PROGRAM. THUS HIS DECISION TO OPEN A HOT DOG STAND ON BUSY 6TH STREET AND RUN FOR MAYOR WAS PERHAPS QUESTIONABLE. AT HIS ANNOUNCEMENT AT WHICH HE REVEALED HIS STATUS, HE WORE AN AMERICAN FLAG AND DRANK BEER FROM A CAN. HE GOT 0.24 PERCENT OF THE VOTE IN 1997.

• PAUL SPRAGENS (A CLOSE FRIEND) RAN FOR CITY COUNCIL IN 1975 WITH A PLATFORM THAT INCLUDED LEGALIZING DUELING, HAVING THE POLICE ALSO SERVE AS A FREE TAXI SERVICE, AND REQUIRING ALL CANDIDATES TO FULLY DISCLOSE THEIR POWER FANTASIES. HE GOT OVER 1,300 VOTES.

• CRAZY CARL HICKERSON (SEE ALSO WEIRD PEOPLE, PAGE 37) USED THE OLD SOVIET ACRONYM CCCP (CRAZY CARL FOR COUNCIL PERSON) IN HIS THREE RUNS FOR COUNCIL FROM 1977 TO 1996. ONE OF HIS FAMED POLITICAL ACTS WAS TO SWIM TO THE MIDDLE OF THEN-TOWN LAKE AND SABOTAGE THE STARTING LIGHTS FOR NOISY SPEEDBOAT RACES IN EAST AUSTIN.

I've seen Crazy Carl and His Man-Boobs - the documentary by Beef and Pie

THIS WAS ONE OF CARL HICKERSON'S MOTTOS IN HIS RUNS FOR COUNCIL. THIS IS A REPRODUCTION CREATED AS A PROMO FOR THE DOCUMENTARY ON HIM GROWING FEMALE-SIZED BREASTS.

• UT STUDENT GOVERNMENT, LONG A WARM-UP FOR ASPIRING POLS, SUCH AS JOHN CONNALLY, JAKE PICKLE, AND LLOYD DOGGETT, HAS HAD PERIODIC APPEARANCES BY WEIRDOS, AT LEAST TWICE SUCCESSFULLY. YOURS TRULY JOINED WITH PALS RICK DAY, DAVID ELDER, AND JOHN WHITE IN 1973 TO ALL RUN SIMULTANEOUSLY FOR STUDENT GOVERNMENT PRESIDENT USING THE SLOGAN "4 FOR TEXAS." WE DIDN'T WIN, INEVITABLY AND FORTUNATELY.

BUT IN 1977 JAY ADKINS AND SKIP SLYFIELD TEAMED UP AS THE ARTS AND SAUSAGES PARTY AND WON. STUDENT GOVERNMENT VOLUNTARILY DISBANDED AT THE END OF THEIR TENURE, SO PROMISE KEPT. IN 2015, STUDENT GOVERNMENT HAVING BEEN RESUSCITATED, TWO OTHER PRANKSTERS WON. PRESUMABLY RUNNING ON THE EYE CHART PARTY, XAVIER ROTNOFSKY AND ROHIT MANDALAPU WON USING THE SLOGAN "WHAT STARTS HERE?" AND SHOWING A MAP OF CALIFORNIA ON THEIR SIGNS.

FORGIVE THE WEIRD

Each Austin City Council session opens with a prayer. Here's an excerpt from the Rev. Vance Russell, who asked for God's help thusly:

I PRAY THAT A SPIRIT OF REPENTANCE COME UPON YOUR PEOPLE FOR BREAKING THEIR RELATIONSHIP WITH YOU. I ASK YOU TO FORGIVE AUSTIN FOR PURSUING FALSE RELIGIONS. FORGIVE US FOR CREATING IDOLS IN PLACE OF WORSHIPING YOU. LORD, YOU ARE JEALOUS OVER AUSTIN. THIS CITY IS NOT WEIRD.

In 2014 Austin switched from having all city council members at large to a ten-district system, which broke the liberal monopoly. Three of the seats went to conservatives of various ilks. A couple of losing candidates were notably wacko. Laura Pressley, despite losing by thirty percentage points, filed endless appeals of the results. Among revelations she brought

out were that Austin Energy's Smart Meters made her legs shake and she could see vibrations from wireless devices. Her briefs were typically over 1,500 pages long. Eventually a judge threw it all out, presumably offended by the assault on the word "brief."

THIS DISTORTION OF THE PHRASE WAS USED IN SOME FORGOTTEN BATTLE OVER SOMETHING OR OTHER.

A high-water mark in our proud claim to be the liberal People's Republic of Austin came in February 2015 when clever lawyer Charles Herring, who has also helped defend notable local weirdness such as the Cathedral of Junk, found a series of short-lived legal loopholes and the first same-sex marriage in Texas took place between Sarah Goodfriend and Suzanne Bryant. This preceded the US Supreme Court's ruling by five months.

SADLY, THIS 2014 CANDIDATE DIDN'T MAKE IT, DESPITE THE IRREFUTABLE LOGIC OF HIS PLATFORM.

A low-water mark in Austin politics happened in 2014 when a lame-duck mayor issued the lamest edict ever, proclaiming December 23, 2014, Red Wassenich Day, thus spoiling Festivus for the rest of us.

IN FEBRUARY 2015, AUSTIN WAS THE SCENE OF THE FIRST SAME-SEX MARRIAGE IN TEXAS WHEN SARAH GOODFRIEND, LEFT, WED SUZANNE BRYANT.

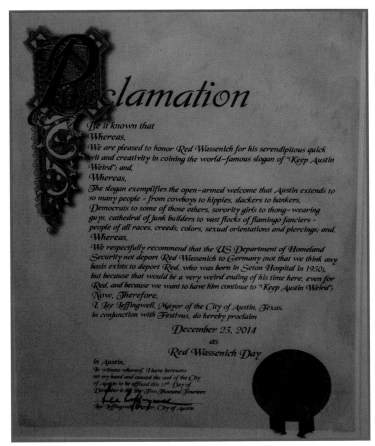

THE ABSOLUTE NADIR OF AUSTIN POLITICS.

CHAPTER 9
WEIRD BUSINESSES

"I BUY AUSTIN"

What's good for general weirdness is good for ATX. As noted in this book's introduction, the popularity of the phrase Keep Austin Weird is largely because of its use by the Austin Independent Business Alliance to promote locally owned businesses. Their official slogan is "I Buy Austin." Specifically it was BookPeople and Waterloo Records at 6th and Lamar who adopted it in their successful fight to end city subsidies of chain stores moving in next door.

Personally I don't really care for shopping as entertainment. I'm a saintly nonmaterialistic sort, but I completely endorse the shop-local approach and this section highlights just a sampling of those who slather on a layer of weirdness to their businesses.

BOOKPEOPLE IS PERENNIALLY VOTED THE BEST BOOKSTORE AND WATERLOO RECORDS AS THE BEST RECORD/CD STORE. MORE IMPORTANT, THEY POPULARIZED THE PHRASE KEEP AUSTIN WEIRD.

THE MUSEUM OF THE WEIRD

In the heart of "Dirty Sixth," the Museum of the Weird is part of the Lucky Lizard art and souvenir store. Two-eyed cyclopses, ghosts in high-thread-count sheets, wisps, and other manifestations of weirdness are on display. Snark aside, this harkens back to sideshows of yore in an entertaining way. 412 E. 6th St., museumoftheweird.com.

SFANTHOR IS FROM THE SAME FOLKS AS LUCKY LIZARD AND MUSEUM OF THE WEIRD. THEY OPENED THIS WAX MUSEUM—HOPE IT'S AIR-CONDITIONED—IN SOCO IN 2015, WHICH WAS IN DIRE NEED OF A CASTLE. IT'S DEDICATED TO CLASSIC HORROR FIGURES. 1101 S. CONGRESS.

SOCO

South Congress is home to dozens of distinctive businesses and many folks consider it the epicenter of Austin weird. There are indeed several great stores, but personally I find most of it too cool for its own good. The displacement of the city's largest food truck compound by a boutique hotel with a "California style" restaurant is exhibit A. But here are some businesses that still make it a worthwhile destination.

LUCY IN DISGUISE WITH DIAMONDS IS A GREAT SOURCE FOR AUSTIN'S FREQUENT NEED FOR COSTUMES AND SWANKY VINTAGE CLOTHES. ITS FACADE ALONE MAKES IT AN ICON. 1506 S. CONGRESS, LUCYINDISGUISE.COM.

UNCOMMON OBJECTS ACCURATELY DESCRIBES ITSELF AS "AN EMPORIUM OF TRANSCENDENT JUNK." IT'S A COLLECTION OF INDIVIDUAL VENDORS, SO THE VARIETY IS OUTSTANDING, AND, HAPPILY, A VEIN OF THE ABSURD RUNS THROUGH IT ALL. BE PREPARED TO SPEND A LONG TIME THERE. 1512 S. CONGRESS, UNCOMMONOBJECTS.COM.

THE AUSTIN MOTEL—AND MUCH OF THE AREA—WAS A LOW-RENT SHADY HANGOUT FOR QUESTIONABLE CHARACTERS UNTIL THE 1980S WHEN DOTTYE DEAN RENOVATED THIS 1938 GEM AND IT BECAME THE ANCHOR FOR HIGH-RENT, SUNGLASSES-WEARING QUESTIONABLE CHARACTERS. THEIR WEBSITE HAS A FASCINATING HISTORY OF IT ALL. 1220 S. CONGRESS, AUSTINMOTEL.COM.

TESOROS IS A SOCO MAINSTAY SINCE IT FLED THE WRECKING BALL ON NORTH CONGRESS. IT'S COMFORTING TO KNOW THERE'S ONE-STOP SHOPPING IN TOWN FOR ASIAN PROPAGANDA KITSCH AND MEXICAN WRESTLER MASKS. 1500 S. CONGRESS.

I ALMOST STOLE THIS SIGN IN SOCO. IT SUMS UP AUSTIN WEIRD IN THREE BUSINESSES: AN ASIAN MEDICINE PRACTITIONER; THE WORLDWIDE INSTITUTE OF SHAMANIC DREAMING, MEDITATION AND METAPHYSICS; AND A CPA.

DEFINITELY NOT IN SOCO

A HALLUCINATION OR THE SIDE YARD OF ROADHOUSE RELICS? YOU DECIDE.

ROADHOUSE RELICS IS DEFINITELY NOT IN SOCO. IT'S ON S. 1ST, DAMN IT. TODD SANDERS, THE OWNER AND ARTIST, SAYS SOCO STANDS FOR "SO CONVENTIONAL." THIS GALLERY IS MAINLY RETRO-NEO-NEON. TODD CREATES NEW WORKS THAT APPEAR OLD. HIS WEBSITE HAS LOTS OF GORGEOUS EXAMPLES AND EXPLANATIONS OF TECHNIQUE. THE AUSTIN MURAL ON THE SIDE (SEE WEIRD ART, PAGE 54) IS AN ICON. 1720 S. 1ST, ROADHOUSERELICS.COM.

ANOTHER S. 1ST BUSINESS, OR WHATEVER IT IS, THAT HIGHLIGHTS ITS NON-SOCO CRED IS SLACKERVILLE, A LOOSE CONFABULATION OF BUSINESSES: SOAP-MAKING, VINYL RECORDS, A JEWELER, A GALLERY, WHO KNOWS WHAT. THIS IS WHERE LAID-BACK GOES ON VACATION. 2209 S. 1ST.

THE BOTTLE HOUSE GALLERY IS AN ANCHOR OF THE SLACKERVILLE ENCLAVE.

THE WHIP IN—JUST YOUR TYPICAL INDIAN GOURMET DELI BREWERY LIVE-MUSIC VENUE WITH A BRING-YOUR-OWN-VINYL BEER GARDEN. THE HOST, DIPAK TOPIWALA, IS THE SELF-DESCRIBED "BEER WALA." THE TAJ MAHAL OF CONVENIENCE STORES. 1950 S. I-35 (WEST ACCESS ROAD), WHIPIN.COM

ELSEWHERE

One of the reassuring aspects of Austin weirdness is that it's not confined to one or two districts secretly managed by the Disney-NSA cabal. It's scattered about nicely. Here's a sampling of our town's far-flung funky businesses.

THE AVENUE B GROCERY & MARKET IS A HIDDEN GEM. IT IS THE "OLDEST CONTINUOUSLY OPERATING GROCERY STORE IN AUSTIN," HAVING BEGUN IN 1909. LOOKING LIKE A PROP FROM THE LAST PICTURE SHOW, IT'S A GREAT EXAMPLE OF THE PLEASURES OF THE HYDE PARK NEIGHBORHOOD—A MIX OF UP- AND DOWN-MARKET. THIS STORE IS MORE OF A SANDWICH SHOP THAN A GROCERY THESE DAYS AND THEIR WARES ARE EXCELLENT. 4403 AVE. B, AVENUEBGROCERY.COM.

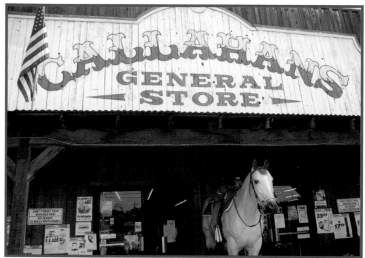

BRASS OVARIES LETS YOU "RELEASE YOUR INNER POLE MONKEY." THE OVARYLESS ARE WELCOMED TOO. SEE BRASS-OVARIES.COM.

CALLAHAN'S GENERAL STORE IS THE IMPORTANT COMBO OF OLD TEXAS AND ODD TEXAS. IT'S BEEN GOING SINCE 1978. HERE YOU'LL FIND A WIDE VARIETY OF LIVE BIRDS, GAUDY WESTERN CLOTHES, WASHBOARDS, RECYCLED-BOTTLE SOY CANDLES, AXE HANDLES, ETC. IT'S HUGE, AND SATURDAY MORNINGS ARE AN ESPECIALLY GOOD TIME TO VISIT: THERE'S ALMOST ALWAYS LIVE MUSIC AND A GOAT PETTING ZOO. 501 S. 183, CALLAHANSGENERALSTORE.COM.

JUST A GIMMICK

As I've fretted before, most probably think Keep Austin Weird is basically a marketing gimmick, so it shouldn't be surprising that it is frequently used as a…marketing gimmick. Here is a sample, literally ripped from the pages of the newspaper.

WE PRESUME THIS MEANS THEY MOW CROP CIRCLES IN YOUR YARD AND CREATE TOPIARY OF RABID BATS.

LEFT: SECOND-BEST MARKETING AWARD GOES TO KEN'S DONUTS ON THE DRAG FOR THIS MURAL OF THE GOD GANESH SPORTING A DONUT.

WALKER TIRES STILL HAS THE BEST MARKETING SLOGAN EVER. TRUE HONESTY IN ADVERTISING. 6208 N. LAMAR.

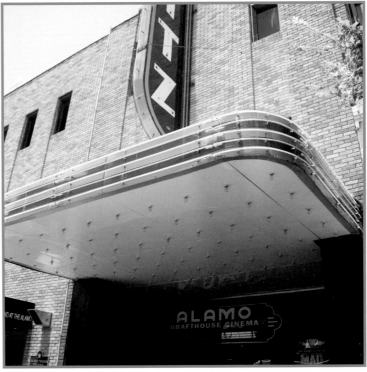

THE ALAMO DRAFTHOUSE MOVIE THEATER FRANCHISE IS ONE OF THE HOTSHOT GO-GETTERS OF AUSTIN WEIRDNESS. THE FIRST PHOTO HERE IS EMBLEMATIC OF ITS GROWTH, ANCHORING THE HUGE NEW LAMAR UNION DEVELOPMENT. WHEN I WROTE MY FIRST BOOK ABOUT AUSTIN WEIRDNESS, IN 2007, IT LOOKED LIKE THE BIZ MIGHT FOLD. BUT NOW, FROM A SINGLE DOWNTOWN THEATER IN 1997 SHOWING SECOND-RUN OFFBEAT FILMS, IT BOASTS OVER FORTY LOCATIONS IN OVER TEN STATES. FOUNDED BY NIGHT-VISIONARIES TIM AND KARRIE LEAGUE, THESE THEATERS PUT RESPECT FOR THE FILM AND THE SERIOUS VIEWER AT THE TOP. OFTEN THE BEST PARTS ARE THE AMAZING COLLECTIONS OF SHORTS SHOWN BEFORE EACH FEATURE. IN AUSTIN, THE RITZ BRANCH ON 6TH STREET HAS THE GOOFIEST MOVIES, WITH WEIRD WEDNESDAY AND FREQUENT SING-ALONGS. MORE AT DRAFTHOUSE.COM.

THE VERY FRIENDLY FOLKS AT AUSTIN'S FURNITURE DEPOT SPECIALIZE IN WEIRD HOME FURNISHINGS. WHO COULDN'T USE A GLADIATOR HELMET FOR THEIR BETTY BOOP NIGHTSTAND? (NOTICE THAT GODZILLA IS EATING DALLAS.) 7511 BURNET RD., AUSTINFURNITUREDEPOT.COM.

HAVING A STORE THAT ONLY SELLS LIGHTBULBS, SUCH AS THE CLEVERLY NAMED LIGHT BULB SHOP, SHOWS THAT EITHER AUSTIN IS SO LARGE IT CAN SUPPORT SUPERSPECIALIZATION OR THAT IT'S JUST ODD. THE WONDERFUL SIGN INDICATES THE LATTER. 6318 BURNET RD.

SOME OF THE BEST VINTAGE SWAG IN TOWN FILLS ROOM SERVICE. IF YOU'RE A CERTAIN AGE, IT'S LIKE A DREAM OF YOUR CHILDHOOD HOME, SO BE PREPARED FOR POSSIBLE TRAUMA OR LAUGHING FITS. CHENILLE BEDSPREAD? CHECK. VELVET BULLFIGHTER PAINTING? CHECK. IN THE ENTERTAINING NORTH LOOP LOCAL BIZ SHOPPING AREA, SO CHECK OUT THE NEIGHBORS. 107 E. NORTH LOOP, ROOMSERVICEVINTAGE.COM.

I WONDER ABOUT THE DEMOGRAPHIC STUDY AT ALLSTATE THAT GOT THIS BILLBOARD APPROVED.

Reagan

Even weirdos like saving money.

Safe drivers save 45% or more

Allstate

1136

LEFT: AN AMUSING SET OF NEXT-DOOR NEIGHBORS IS THE NEWISH MALVERN BOOKS AND THE OLDISH OAT WILLIES. THE FORMER IS A SLEEK ENCLAVE PROMOTING POETRY AND OFTEN ESOTERIC FICTION FROM INDEPENDENT PUBLISHERS, WHILE THE LATTER IS A HEAD SHOP THAT'S BEEN GOING SINCE THE 1960S. THIS WOULD MAKE A GREAT SITCOM, À LA THE ODD COUPLE. ONWARD THROUGH THE FOG! 613 AND 617 W. 29TH ST., MALVERNBOOKS.COM AND OATWILLIES.COM.

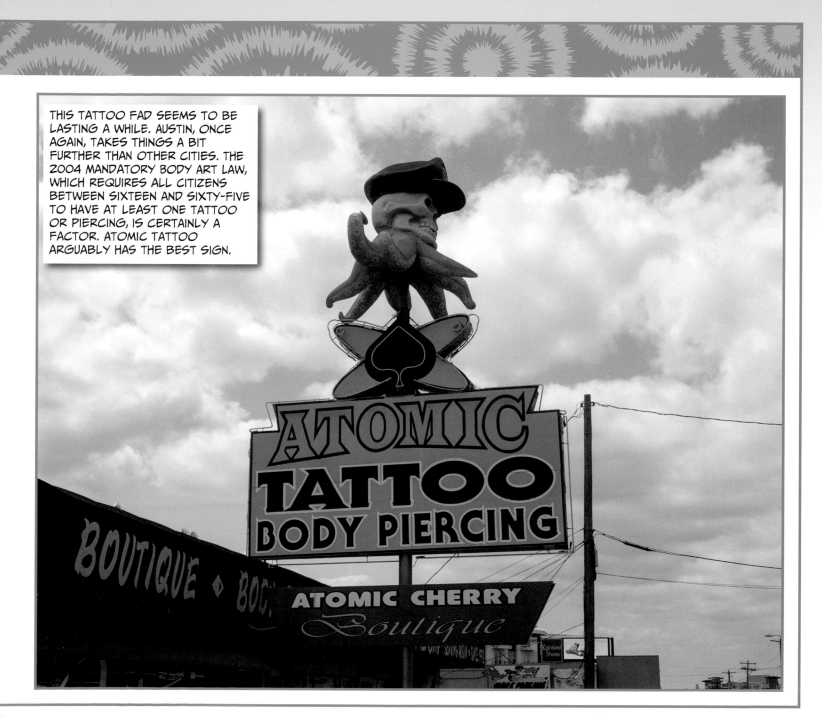

THIS TATTOO FAD SEEMS TO BE LASTING A WHILE. AUSTIN, ONCE AGAIN, TAKES THINGS A BIT FURTHER THAN OTHER CITIES. THE 2004 MANDATORY BODY ART LAW, WHICH REQUIRES ALL CITIZENS BETWEEN SIXTEEN AND SIXTY-FIVE TO HAVE AT LEAST ONE TATTOO OR PIERCING, IS CERTAINLY A FACTOR. ATOMIC TATTOO ARGUABLY HAS THE BEST SIGN.

ATOMIC
TATTOO
BODY PIERCING

BOUTIQUE • BOU

ATOMIC CHERRY
Boutique

HIS BOWTIE IS REALLY A CAMERA. AT THE AUSTIN SPY SHOP YOU CAN FIND THAT AND ALL SORTS OF INTRIGUING CLANDESTINE DEVICES AND SOME MILITANT LIBERTARIAN TCHOTCHKES TOO. THE FRIENDLY FOLKS WHO RUN IT, LYNDON LEUDERS AND KIVA MCDONALD, CAN EXPLAIN IT AND GIVE YOU A GLIMPSE INTO A WORLD YOU WEREN'T SURE EXISTED. 1003 E. 53RD ST., AUSTINSPYSHOP.COM.

THE NUMEROUS PIÑATA STORES IN EAST AUSTIN, ALWAYS A COLORFUL TREAT, GAINED PROMINENCE DURING SXSW 2015 FOR TWO VERY DISPARATE REASONS. ON THE BRIGHT SIDE, JIMMY KIMMEL, WHO MOVES HIS NIGHTLY CHAT SHOW HERE DURING THE FESTIVAL, DID A FUNNY DRINKING GAME AT MULTIPLE STORES, WHILE ON THE DARK SIDE, A CORPORATE A-HOLE STOLE ONE STORE'S SPOT, SENDING OUT A TEAM THAT DEMOLISHED EVERYTHING WITHOUT WARNING, JUST SO HE COULD RENT THE VACANT LOT FOR A SXSW UNOFFICIAL EVENT. WHEN WORD GOT OUT, A BOYCOTT OF THE COMPANY QUICKLY CAUSED THE CANCELLATION OF THE EVENT AND THE DIMWIT CEO RESPONSIBLE WAS BOOTED.

IN ADDITION TO A GREAT DINER BREAKFAST, BURGERS, AND FOUNTAIN DRINKS, NAU'S HAS ALL YOUR CANDY CIGARETTE AND FART TOY NEEDS.

NAU'S ENFIELD DRUG EARNS ITS WEIRDNESS BONA FIDES ON AT LEAST TWO LEVELS: IT'S 1956 INSIDE, WITH A CLASSIC SODA FOUNTAIN DISPENSING HAND-BUILT MALTS 'N' BURGERS, AND THEIR COLLECTION OF ODD TOYS AND CANDY. IT'S A NIFTY GATHERING SPOT OF NEIGHBORHOOD REGULARS. THE EX-DALLAS COWBOY HOLLYWOOD HENDERSON WON $28 MILLION IN THE LOTTERY FROM A TICKET PURCHASED AT NAU'S, SO THEY GOT A BIG BONUS. THE NEIGHBORHOOD FEARFULLY AWAITED A RUINOUS MAKEOVER. ALL THAT HAPPENED WAS THEY SWITCHED FROM A MECHANICAL CASH REGISTER TO AN ELECTRONIC ONE. W. 12TH ST. & WEST LYNN ST., NAUSDRUG.COM.

VULCAN VIDEO HAS BEEN PROVIDING ACCESS TO VHSS AND DVDS SINCE 1990, SPECIALIZING IN ODDITIES AND ESOTERICA. THEY ARRANGE THEIR WARES IN FAMOUSLY SPECIALIZED CATEGORIES, SUCH AS CANADIAN TV AND FORMER YUGOSLAVIA. IN 2015 JIMMY KIMMEL'S LATE-NIGHT SHOW BROADCAST FROM AUSTIN FOR A WEEK AND HAD A CONTEST TO DO A COMMERCIAL FOR A LOCAL BUSINESS. VULCAN WON AND KIMMEL AND LOCAL BOY MATTHEW MCCONAUGHEY DID THREE VERY FUNNY ONES, WHICH ARE, OF COURSE, ON YOUTUBE. 112 W. ELIZABETH ST. & 100 A NORTH LOOP, VULCANVIDEO.COM.

IN WHAT WAS NO DOUBT A WRENCHING CORPORATE DECISION, VULCAN MERGED ITS GODZILLA AND KAIJU COLLECTION WITH ITS JAPAN HOLDINGS.

MANAGER BRYAN CONNOLLY IN VULCAN VIDEO'S HUGE COLLECTION OF ANTIQUE VHS TAPES.

RED WASSENICH COINED THE PHRASE "KEEP AUSTIN WEIRD" IN 2000. HE WAS BORN IN AUSTIN AND HAS BEEN A LIBRARIAN AT AUSTIN COMMUNITY COLLEGE SINCE 1984. WHILE NOW LIVING A SEEMINGLY NORMAL LIFE, HIS PAST SHOWS THE ROOTS OF WEIRDNESS. HE AND PAUL SPRAGENS AND OTHERS BROADCAST ON MEXICAN RADIO BORDER-BLASTER STATION XEG THE "BROTHER HEUMANN HOUR," STARRING A PARODY EVANGELIST FROM THE CHURCH OF THE COINCIDENTAL METAPHOR. ALSO WITH SPRAGENS, HE WATCHED TV FOR A WEEK FROM SIGN-ON TO SIGN-OFF (BACK WHEN THERE USED TO BE SUCH A THING). HE PLAYED A CADAVER IN THE MOVIE *THE HUNGER* WITH DAVID BOWIE AND CATHERINE DENEUVE. HE IS NOW HAPPILY MARRIED TO KAREN PAVELKA.